31 DAYS OF WHOLENESS

WOMEN'S DAILY DEVOTIONAL/WORKBOOK

DR. SHARON SMITH-KOEN

WOMEN'S DAILY DEVOTIONAL/WORKBOOK

31 Days Of Wholeness

First Printing: 2016

ISBN 9781541391390

PUBLISHING

We Help Make Visions Come True!

Info at: rhemapublishing1@gmail.com

TABLE OF CONTENTS

ACKNOWLEDGMENT

I have compiled these 31 days of scriptures to encourage my sisters in the Lord to experience the wholeness of God, no matter what they may go through from day to day. I have incorporated some of my own testimonies, along with the testimonies of some mighty women of God that I have met along the way. It is my hope that you will read this inspirational devotional over and over and gain strength for the journey. I say thank you to the women who wholeheartedly shared testimonies so others could become whole.

"And they overcame and conquered him because of the blood of the Lamb and because of the word of their testimony, for they did not love their life and renounce their faith even when faced with death." Revelation
12:11

Be Blessed and Be Whole,   Love Sharon

Day 1

Trials and Temptations Bring Wholeness

James 1:1-5

*"James, a servant of God and the Lord Jesus Christ, to
the twelve tribes scattered among the nations: Consider
it pure joy, my brothers, whenever you face <u>trials</u> of
many kinds because you know that the testing of your
faith develops perseverance. Perseverance must finish its
work so that you may be <u>mature</u> and <u>complete,</u> not
lacking anything. If any of you lacks wisdom, he should
ask God, who gives generously to all without finding
fault, and it will be given to him".*

James speaks here as a leader in the Jerusalem church and the brother of Jesus. However, in his humility he did not write based on either one of these aspects but referred to himself as a servant. He writes to the twelve tribes of Jews living in many parts of the world who had become Christians. His teaching is for all Christians then and now exhorting us to believe and do what God requires, regardless of the circumstances. In his exhortation, he explains that trials can be a real test of our trust in Almighty God. However, as we overcome each trial, they will accomplish what God desires in our lives, bringing us to a place of ultimate wholeness.

The Greek word for trials is **peirasmos** which make reference to persecution and difficulties that emanate from Satan and the world. It is incumbent on the believer who wants to experience wholeness to develop durable faith, and maturity, in an effort to experience true wholeness. James refers to these trials as a "testing of your faith". In essence, sometimes God will test the genuineness of our faith to move us into a new arena of wholeness. This does not mean God is displeased with us but could be an indication that He recognizes our solid dedication to Him. Trials cause us to have to depend on God and ultimately draw us closer to Him. The Biblical maturity that is emphasized here is reflected by a true connection with God where the believer is continuously bearing fruit and exhibiting a passionate love for God. This is a wholehearted commitment to the Lover of our souls. These verses also mention the word wisdom and this word in Proverbs is usually referred to in the context of a woman. Thus wisdom is referred to as she. It is a revelation of existence and thoughts based on God's blueprint. The realization here is that nothing is worth more than attaining God's wisdom and when we do we live in light of His perfect will which always comes with a measure of affliction.

Prior to the birth of my second grandchild, I watched as my daughter persevered through a very difficult pregnancy. She currently lives in San Diego and when I visited some months before and listened as the doctors explained all that was going on with her unborn child, I marveled at her trust in God. They basically told her this would be a complex situation, and they seemed unsure as to whether she would get through the next few months. She, however, chose to believe the report of the Lord which said her baby would be healed. I am sure she inspired many when she wrote on Facebook with a heart of thanksgiving to those who have been interceding in prayer for her and her family. These were

her words: "I just want to take this time to say that my

daughter has truly been kept by God and Him alone. All

my doctors thought she would not make it, but when

you serve a God like mine the impossible is made

possible. My faith has been tested in these past months

and I have been made stronger. I have sewn my seed

and I am ready to rejoice in my harvest. Thank you

Jesus"! What a testimony; the battle continued but as I

continued preparing to go to California for the birth of

my granddaughter I recognized that this was an

example of experiencing wholeness in the midst of trials.

As I sat in the airport waiting to board the plane

for San Diego on July 18, 2015, my daughter called

numerous times giving me a play by play of how they

were inducing labor so her baby could be born one

month early, not wanting her to go to full term. As I

boarded the first plane I hoped that I would make it in

time for the delivery, and prayed that she would have a

safe birth, considering all the agony she endured having

to visit the hospital at least three times a week for most

of the pregnancy. As I was about to board the second

plane, I listened as she told me how much pain she was

in, with her voice quivering so much I could hardly

decipher what she was saying. As the plane landed in

San Diego I received word that she had given birth to

princess Leilani weighing 4 lbs. 7 oz. I was taken

directly from the airport to the hospital. I would spend

the next five days waiting for news that our baby girl was

able to go home. As I watched my daughter get out of

bed every three hours, and walk the halls of the hospital

to the NICU to feed her baby, I recognized this had

taken a toll on her. I also recognized a warrior spirit who

realized no matter how hard the trial, if she trusted God

she would be victorious and whole every time.

~Sharon~

It is my prayer that no matter what trial you may be going through in this season, that you will take solace in the fact that in persevering you will become mature and complete. Persevering faith is what builds warriors in the kingdom. Though it may seem like God has forgotten you, He has not. He is working it out but requires you to endure so He can get glory from your experience. Hold fast my sisters, this too will pass and you will come forth whole.

HAVE A BLESSED DAY!!!

Day 1 Study Questions

How does this scripture tap into your understanding of

trials bringing wholeness?

_____

_____

_____

_____

_____

_____

_____

_____

_____

_____

_____

_____

_____

What are some trials that you currently face? How can

you utilize them to make you whole?

_____

_____

_____

_____

_____

_____

_____

_____

_____

_____

_____

_____

_____

_____

How does today's testimony strengthen you in your walk

with the Lord?

_____

_____

_____

_____

_____

_____

_____

_____

_____

_____

_____

_____

_____

_____

_____

Day 2

Triumph over the Thief Brings Wholeness

John 10:10

"The thief comes only to steal and kill and destroy; I am come that they may have life, and have it to the full".

Webster defines a thief as one who steals; one who commits theft or larceny; a waster. The Biblical definition of a thief is one coming without warning (Matthew 24:43); a wrongdoer as the thief crucified with Christ (Luke 23:32 and 39). The Greek word **kleptes** = a thief and lestes = a robber. In John 10:10, Jesus not only discusses the thief but introduces Himself as the Good Shepherd, explaining to the Pharisees His role as the Messiah. The Greek word used here for a thief is defined as one who enters a house to steal (their next inclination, if discovered is to kill and destroy the owner of the house).

In this Biblical reference for today's devotion, we need an understanding of who this thief is that is being talked about. In our Christian circles, we identify him as Satan, who was once an archangel called Lucifer. He wanted to replace God in Heaven so he could be worshiped instead. Therefore, God showed up in His power and expelled Satan and the angels under his leadership from heaven, as a result of their disloyalty. Thus, we recognize him as a thief and a destroyer. Hence, as we observe this thief Jesus is referring to here in John 10:10, we realize that He is making reference to those who falsely teach, and proclaim to preach God's Word. They are in fact instruments of Satan being utilized in the house of God, and believers sit around embracing their words as truth, thus being deceived by Satan himself. We, as God's children, must recognize that it takes only a minute quantity of Biblical blunder to bring destruction. By adhering to the words of these false teachers, and preachers, we gradually become demolished, torn down, and at times become spiritually and emotionally dead.

The devil seems to be gaining an advantage over the sophisticated Church on so many levels. One of these is by stealing our peace and joy daily. Therefore, it's time for us to take our rightful place, go into his domain and declare "back off, enough is enough, you lose". In John 8:31-32 Jesus declares *"if you hold to my teaching you are really my disciples. Then you will know the truth, and the truth will set you free"*. There is only one inerrant truth that exists, and it is the pure unadulterated Word of God. This truth has the power to set us free from sin, and the devastation of Satan's dominance. This truth that sets us free and makes us whole does not originate in man's wisdom but in the wisdom of almighty God.

Thus, we conclude that there is a thief on the loose, and the Bible tells us in 1Peter 5:8 to *"be self-controlled and alert, because our enemy the devil, prowls around like a roaring lion, looking for someone to devour"*. We, therefore, cannot allow ourselves to be deceived into thinking

he will not use any and everything he can to destroy us. As a
roaring lion, although we have been delivered from his
power, he continues to be a menace. He seeks to destroy us,
especially through experiences of trials and suffering.
However, through spiritual warfare we can arm ourselves
with the weapons at our disposal described in Ephesians
6:10-18, and be fully outfitted to crush Satan's schemes. We
cannot allow this thief to wreak havoc in our lives by taking
homes, jobs, families, ministries, marriages etc., thus, feeling
satisfied he has stolen our peace. In an effort to gain
wholeness we must get angry enough to fight, in an effort to
recapture what this thief has had the audacity to steal from us.
The apostle Paul in Philippians 3:13-14 admonishes *"forget
what is behind, and strain toward what is ahead,
pressing on toward the goal to win the prize for which
God has called us heavenward in Christ Jesus.*

HAVE A BLESSED DAY!!!

Day 2 Study Questions

How is the enemy infiltrating your territory today?

_____

_____

_____

_____

_____

_____

_____

_____

_____

_____

_____

_____

_____

_____

_____

Is there an area of your life where Satan seems stronger than others? If so which area?

_____

_____

_____

_____

_____

_____

_____

_____

_____

_____

_____

_____

_____

_____

How can you use the weaponry in Ephesians 6 to

destroy Satan and take your life back?

_____

_____

_____

_____

_____

_____

_____

_____

_____

_____

_____

_____

_____

_____

_____

_____

Day 3

Reconciliation Brings Wholeness

2 Corinthians 5:17-19

"Therefore, if anyone is in Christ, he is a new creation; the old has gone, the new has come! All this is from God, who <u>reconciled</u> us to himself through Christ and gave us the ministry of <u>reconciliation</u>: that God was <u>reconciling</u> the world to himself in Christ, not counting men's sins against them. And He has committed to us the <u>message of reconciliation</u>.

The Bible explains here that as a result of God's original dominion when we accept Christ by faith we become new and totally belong to God. We, therefore, are given a special place in His new world with the Holy Spirit as our ruler. We are transformed into God's likeness, thus, having an allotment in His splendor. This is an awesome renewal because it gives us new understanding and knowledge, and the ability to live truly holy lives. We are admonished here by Paul the apostle, to get rid of the old baggage that we once carried in the world of sin. This baggage weighed us down, causing us to be susceptible to the demonic forces that had us bound.

Although we are given this mandate and a host of examples

and scriptures to feed our spirits, we still find ourselves

succumbing to the errors of our old ways. I believe Paul, in

his admonition, is echoing the words the prophet stated in

Isaiah 43:18-19 which said *"forget the former things, do*

not dwell on the past. See I am doing a new thing!"

Hence, this is a reminder of how we should live as a result of

this gift of new life bestowed on us by our heavenly Father.

In these verses we see the word reconcile in different

forms. Reconciliation in the Greek is **katallage**, and is one

attribute of the redemptive work of Christ. It is as a result of

this reconciling that our companionship with God is restored.

The sin and revolt that we experienced while estranged from

God in the world, made us antagonistic toward God and His

Word. God, however, as a result of His unconditional love,

has made a way for us to return to God. This, however,

requires repentance on our part, and genuine faith in God.

The Bible declares in Romans 5:8 *"God demonstrates His own love for us in this: While we were still sinners, Christ died for us."* God didn't wait for us to repent but gave His only Son when we were still living in sin. WHAT LOVE!!!

I recall the first time I experienced the reconciling power of God. I was only ten years old and I heard my sister, who is twelve years my senior, talking about Jesus over and over. My parents had sent her to a Bible believing and teaching Sunday school and she went religiously. When she received Christ as Savior, she came home, and like the Samaritan woman at the well in John chapter 4, she told me and the rest of her family to come see a Man. Eventually, I believe those words changed our family, from the youngest to the oldest, and she continues to be a witness to His reconciling power. Though, as a result of wrong choices in my teenage and young adult years, I revisited the world and its pleasures,

I eventually resolved to let old things pass away and all things become new. That decision has permitted me to experience a newness of life that is hard to explain. Even during times of adversity, suffering, and trials, when at times I couldn't and still can't see the handwriting on the wall, I knew and continue to know I can experience wholeness if I stay in a place of making all things new.
~Sharon~

This mandate becomes difficult when we ignore this command, seeking rather to compromise with the world. The Bible explains in Psalm 1 the two types of people (godly and ungodly). Therefore, all things become new when we choose to be godly. This person is promised blessing because he/she chooses not to walk in the way of the ungodly but seeks rather to delight in God's law. This person, because of his/her perseverance, is given the same growth ability of a "tree planted by streams of water". This tells us that our choice to live godly reaps benefits for us, allowing us to grow

and become whole.

HAVE A BLESSED DAY!!!

Day 3 Study Questions

Are you carrying baggage that is wearing you down and keeping you from wholeness? If yes how can you start releasing them today?

_____

_____

_____

_____

_____

_____

_____

_____

_____

_____

_____

_____

_____

_____

What are some old things that you have brought into

your new life that keeps you from experiencing real

reconciliation?

_____

_____

_____

_____

_____

_____

_____

_____

_____

_____

_____

_____

_____

What are some compromises with the world, that when relinquished will render you completely whole?

_____

_____

_____

_____

_____

_____

_____

_____

_____

_____

_____

_____

_____

_____

Day 4

Renewed Minds Bring Wholeness

Romans 12:1-2

"Therefore, I urge you, brothers, in view of God's mercy, to offer your bodies as living sacrifices, holy and pleasing to God—this is your spiritual act of worship. Do not conform any longer to the pattern of this world, but be transformed by the renewing of your mind. Then you will be able to test and approve what God's will is— His good, pleasing and perfect will"

After Paul the apostle takes the time in the first eleven chapters of Romans conducting deep rooted religious studies, he transitions into this chapter with heartfelt words concerning how we, as believers, ought to live. He exhorts us to take the doctrine off the page and begin to flesh it out in our lives. This chapter exudes with more than exhortations but commands about the condition of our lifestyles. This is one of the greatest calls to action in the New Testament. Verse 1 is referred to by most commentaries as one of the most important in scripture. It explains what we should do in reaction to what God the Father did in sending His Son to die for us. As authors, we generally use the word "therefore" to explain what we have said previously. Paul is no different in his writing, in that his "therefore" here explains what the previous set of guidelines in chapter 1 to 11 is "there for". It expresses the fact that we ought to do more than just hear the Word but do it. James 1:22 explains it best when it says *"Do not merely listen to the Word and so deceive yourselves. Do what it says"*. As believers, we are born again as a result of the Word, and when we start doing the Word, we practice what we learn.

Verse 1 of Romans 12 gives a directive to make a sacrificial presentation of our entire bodies back to God. One songwriter says it best with the lyrics "you provide the fire, and I will provide the sacrifice". The first time I heard that song, it took me back to the event of Abraham's willingness to present his son Isaac as a sacrifice in Genesis 22, knowing this was the promised seed for future generations. God, however, provided a ram as the substitute. This depiction revealed to God the willingness of Abraham, and his main concern to do God's will. We have to determine to make worship a sacrificial part of who we are. It is fairly easy to enter into worship on Sunday morning when all the saints gather in the sanctuary. I believe the real sacrifice occurs Monday to Saturday when all hell is breaking loose in our lives. We have to make a conscious effort today to make this weekly sacrifice of worship to God, no matter what it looks like, or feels like. We must daily devote ourselves to talk to God who is Abba (Daddy), Almighty, Lover of our souls and so much more. He deserves a daily sacrifice of praise and worship, not just for what He does, but most importantly for who He is.

In verse 2 of Romans 12, Paul explains how this sacrificial life is to be attained. It all begins in the mind; therefore, he exhorts us to renew our minds. You may be asking at this moment, how do I do that when there is chaos all around me? The idea, according to Paul, is not to remain in conformity to this world. We have to remember that this world is our temporary home; therefore, our conformity should be to living wholly for God. The Greek word for conformity used here is **suschematizo**, which means to be molded or stamped according to a pattern. Thus, if we allow ourselves to be branded and stamped by this world we will conform to it. However, when we refuse to let the world's standards give us a stamp of approval and instead let God mold us and stamp His seal of approval on us, we become supernaturally whole.

As I take inventory of my life I recognize those defining moments as when I stretched out in faith and allowed Almighty God to transform me. I recall one special instance as He hacked away at those things that had to dissipate in order for Him to get full control. There were times when all I could say was "OUCH" because it hurt so much. He, in turn, said "Sharon, my daughter, I want to transform and use you in ways that you can't even imagine, but in order to do that I have to get rid of some undesirable things in your life. After flinching and fussing for a little while I stood at attention and said, with tears rolling down my face, "I surrender all". This was one of many defining moments when I released all the baggage and allowed wholeness to take over so I could be FREE.

~Sharon~

I pray this day finds all my sisters in a position where they are able to be sacrificial in presenting their entire being to their Creator. I pray that your minds will be set free to think whole thoughts, but that can only be done if you set your face like flint towards God, serving Him wholeheartedly so you can experience real wholeness.

HAVE A BLESSED DAY!!!

Day 4 Study Questions

How are you doing the Word today?

_____

_____

_____

_____

_____

_____

_____

_____

_____

_____

_____

_____

_____

_____

_____

How will you give God a sacrifice of praise today?

_____

_____

_____

_____

_____

_____

_____

_____

_____

_____

_____

_____

_____

_____

**What are some things that God is removing to get full
control of your life?**

_____

_____

_____

_____

_____

_____

_____

_____

_____

_____

_____

_____

_____

_____

_____

Day 5

Pruning by the Master Brings Wholeness

John 15:1-8

"I am the true vine, and My Father is the vinedresser. Every branch in me that does not bear fruit He takes away and every branch that bears fruit He prunes, that it may bear more fruit. You are already clean because of the word which I have spoken to you. Abide in Me, and I in you. As the branch cannot bear fruit of itself, unless it abides in the vine, neither can you, unless you abide in Me. "I am the vine, you are the branches. He who abides in me, and I in him, bears much fruit; for without me you can do nothing. If anyone does not abide in me, he is cast out as a branch and is withered; and they gather them and throw them into the fire, and they are burned. If you abide in me, and my words abide in you, you will ask what you desire, and it shall be done for you. By this My Father is glorified, that you bear much fruit; so you will be my disciples".

Jesus calls Himself the true vine because there are counterfeit vines (job, education, family, money etc.). No one can claim spiritual inheritance through these. God's original vine was Israel, but they fell because of disobedience. They became obsessed with the worldly things around them and bore no fruit. It is only through Christ that one becomes a part of the true vineyard and lineage of God. Some Biblical scholars say the fruitless

branches are unbelievers, while others say they are Christians

who bear no fruit.

Vines usually require regular pruning by the gardener

to keep them healthy, attractive, under control and

productive. Many vines, if left to themselves, won't know

when to quit, or in which direction to grow. There must be

consistent cutting away. Pruning doesn't just remove

unwanted leaves and give direction but encourages new

growth. It is an incessant process of removing dead,

damaged, diseased and unproductive stems. There must be an

elimination of overly tangled stems, like shackles that tangle

our feet and make us unable to dance. There must be the

removal of stems that grow away from the vine. Jesus wants

to bear fruit through us, but we can't bear fruit if we grow

away from Him. We have to ask ourselves; what are some

dead, damaged and diseased things that need to be detached

so we can grow.

This discourse between Jesus and the disciples began
in chapter 14 where He comforts them, knowing He was
about to die. He reassured them that He wouldn't leave them
alone, but would send the Holy Spirit as the Comforter.
Though Jesus was speaking to all twelve disciples, He knew
only eleven were truly faithful and truly listening and Judas
would betray Him. In this dialogue He saw eleven disciples,
whom He loved dearly; He saw the Father with whom He
shared an endless love; but He grieved over Judas who He
loved in spite of. In spite of all his foolishness and ultimate
betrayal, that would transpire. Here in chapter 15 Jesus is
telling his disciples how they and all believers after them are
required to live. The basis of the message is: if we abide in
Him, and allow Him to abide in us, we will bear much fruit.
The essence of the discourse is WITHOUT CONSTANT
PRUNING and WITHOUT HIM WE CAN DO
NOTHING. Jesus has to be at the center of all we do, there
can be no mediocrity and half stepping; there can be no wishy

washy connection. We have to trust Him all the way even when it looks impossible, there can be no backup plan. God gives us one master plan in Jeremiah 29:11 declaring *"For I know the plans and thoughts I have for you, says the Lord, plans for peace and well-being and not for disaster; to give you a future and a hope"*.

Judas and all who are not really connected, become fruitless branches. Judas appeared to be like the other eleven and he was with Jesus the same amount of time; he was even made treasurer. We must be careful not to get caught up in the titles and roles we play, without having a genuine connection. Judas seemed to be a branch like the others, but never bore real fruit and had to be cut off and burned. We have to be careful not to have a phoney connection, realizing that Judas branches exist in all churches. God is looking for true disciples of all church ages who have total trust in Him, total faith in Him, know their purpose and know how to produce fruit. It is only when we allow Him to prune us that

we grow and become whole.

HAVE A BLESSED DAY!!!

Day 5 Study Questions

**What are some dead areas in your life that need to be
removed to bring wholeness?**

_____

_____

_____

_____

_____

_____

_____

_____

_____

_____

_____

_____

_____

_____

_____

_____

How does knowing that pruning will eventually bring

growth help you stand up to it?

_____

_____

_____

_____

_____

_____

_____

_____

_____

_____

_____

_____

_____

_____

How can you prevent yourself from becoming a fruitless

branch in the kingdom?

_____

_____

_____

_____

_____

_____

_____

_____

_____

_____

_____

_____

_____

Day 6

A Spirit of Contentment Brings Wholeness

Philippians 4:11-13

Not that I speak in regard to need, for I have learned in whatever state I am, to be content: I know how to be abased, and I know how to abound. Everywhere and in all things I have learned both to be full and to be hungry, both to abound and to suffer need. I can do all things through Christ who strengthens me.

The Greek word for contentment here is **autarkés** which means self-sufficient, contented, satisfied and independent. Paul states that he has learned to be satisfied in any condition, even after all the suffering he had endured. He recognized that the circumstances of life that God sometimes allows, although they at times require suffering, will result in contentment if we endure. Paul explains that he has endured seasons of hunger and seasons of plenty, yet he has learned how to be content regardless of the situation. He continues the dialogue by emphasizing that he and all who make a declaration of faith in God can do all things through Christ

who gives us the strength.

As I continue my pursuit for Godliness and

holiness I must reflect on those periods of lack when I

thought I would not make it. I recall driving to the ATM

machine at times with my children and praying that God

would miraculously provide the funds I needed to pay

my bills. I think in those times I was looking for God to

be a magician and not the miracle working God that He

is. It was during those seasons that this scripture

became reality for me. I would cry out to God morning,

noon and night and I think this is when He truly

became Abba for me. I lost my earthly father in 1995, but

I remember depending on him for just about everything.

He referred to me as his "heart string" and even when

times were financially difficult for him I never knew it,

because he always found a way to help me and others.

Galatians 4:6 explains "because you are sons, God has

sent forth the Spirit of His Son into your hearts, crying

out, "Abba, Father!" Abba is Aramaic and it means

Father and Jesus used it to refer to the heavenly Father.

It encompasses deep emotion and intimacy which is

how our heavenly Father wants us to embrace Him.

These all-consuming words in Galatians gives me and

all believers the assurance of knowing that Daddy God

will never let us go hungry, but He will supply for every

need and just wants us to rest in that promise. In

essence, while I loved my earthly daddy with all my

heart, my heavenly Daddy is the only one that can

supply for me always. I learned that in those times of

desperate need, as He continuously performed miracles

in providing for me and my children.

I learned, like Paul, that "everywhere and in all

things how to be full and hungry, both to abound and to

suffer need". This was very daunting at times because I

never knew when, where or how it would all work

together. However, what I learned during all those hours

of prayer and fasting was God wanted me to be content.

After a while, I found that worrying couldn't resolve

anything because my Daddy was doing His thing and

He wanted me to let go and let Him take control. I

learned how to rely on His strength because mine was

zapped. Worry turned into contentment as I lived my

moment by moment life with the One who loved me

best. Though the needs mounted, God showed up on

every terrain and showed me that I could do ALL things

through Him who gives me strength.

~Sharon~

Paul explained to his protégé Timothy that

"Godliness with contentment is great gain. For we

brought nothing into the world, and we can take nothing

out of it". (1Timothy 6:6-7) He also went on to say we need

to be content with the essentials of life like food. How many

of us, if we were to be truly honest, would be able to say that we are content with the bare necessities of life? One commentary on this verse states "Every earthly possession is only meant for this life—for the period between the hour of birth and the hour of death; we entered this world with nothing, we shall leave the world again with nothing. If we could take anything with us when death parts soul and body there would at once be an end to the "contentment".

Therefore, since we realize we can take nothing with us as we sojourn through this pathway called life, we need to take introspection every day recognizing that God owes us nothing and we, therefore, need to be content. As I started my journaling in January 2016 I found myself writing at the beginning, every day, how thankful I am to God for another day of life. I recognize more than ever that I am truly blessed for the mere fact that I am breathing, have all my faculties and all is well with my health. I say today to you my sisters and comrades seek to develop a spirit of contentment with such things that you have, realizing this will bring you

wholeness.

HAVE A BLESSED DAY!!!

Day 6 Study Questions

How does knowing you are a child of the King bring

contentment?

_____

_____

_____

_____

_____

_____

_____

_____

_____

_____

_____

_____

_____

Are you honestly content with the bare necessities of

life? If not what will it take for real contentment to

occur?

_____

_____

_____

_____

_____

_____

_____

_____

_____

_____

_____

_____

_____

_____

How does Philippians 4:11-13 give you a new outlook on

contentment?

_____

_____

_____

_____

_____

_____

_____

_____

_____

_____

_____

_____

_____

Day 7

Trusting in God Brings Wholeness

Proverbs 3:5-6

"Trust in the Lord with all your heart, and lean not on your own understanding; in all your ways acknowledge Him, and He shall direct your paths".

The fragment of this verse that always speaks volumes to me is "in all your ways". Thus, regardless of the pitfalls and stumbling blocks, we must remain undaunted in our trust. When life shows up with its twists and turns and all hell is breaking loose all around **we must trust**. When the devil eats away at us like he oft times does **we must trust**. When the bills are high and funds are low **we must trust**. When life seems unfair and we cannot see beyond the trees **we must trust**. When it seems we are alone with nothing or no one to comfort **we must trust**. When that loved one is taken in the prime of life **we must trust**. When sickness ensues and doctors quit **we must trust**. In essence, trust must be the

trademark of the believer's life.

In my career as an adjunct professor, I have had the

opportunity to meet some very awesome students. I walked

into Palm Beach Atlantic University during one of the

summer semesters and met a woman that I will not soon

forget. When asked to introduce herself, she boldly told the

class she was 64 years old with a mission to succeed in her

academic career. Immediately I held her in great esteem and

now you have the occasion to read part of her testimony.

In all of Solomon's wisdom, he gave

instructions to his son that said, "Trust in the Lord with

all your heart, and do not lean on your own

understanding. In all your ways acknowledge Him, and

He will make straight your paths" (Proverbs 3:5-6 ESV).

These are instructions that one may find easier to

verbalize than actually achieve. Life has a strange way of

teaching us the truths of God's word; the importance of

surrendering our will or what we think we understand

about life. In order to trust God when there seems to be

no sane reason to have confidence, there is hope to

overcome the present day circumstance. The Bible

declares that everyone has been given a "measure of

faith" and without faith, no matter how large or small

the measure, it is "impossible to please God." My

learning to trust God with every ounce of faith I had did

not come easy, but, rather it tested every fiber of my

heart, pulled at every nerve in my body, and brought me

to a point of total praise to and faith in God, and my

Lord and Savior Jesus Christ.

After retiring from my job in 2010, for the first

time in my adult life I was able to have the resources to

live the life I had only dreamed of; one where I didn't

have to make a choice of what was more important to

buy, or what bill to pay. However, that luxury was short

lived and my nightmare started in May 2011 and by

September 2012, I found myself at the point of foreclosure and possible homelessness. There was no logical explanation of how I got to this dark alley in my life, but God, being fully aware of what was ahead for me, challenged me to hold fast to the instructions of Proverbs 3:5-6. Was God saying, "Trust in Me and do not try to understand what you are going through"? Did God know the people at the bank didn't care whether I believed in Him or not? What I remember saying to God was, "This is beyond me, but, nevertheless at your word I will trust you", but it did not come without tears.

At one point I felt lifeless and like a failure. Every negative thing I had been told about my life in the area of my finances seemed to plague my mind. When I applied for the Federal Mortgage Hardship Assistance Program, I was told I didn't qualify at the time, but the program was being revised and I could re-apply later. After talking with a friend whose non-profit assisted

residents with such problems, I re-applied following the
directions on what to write on the application. One day
in early August 2012 I received my first Notice of Intent
to file for foreclosure, and shortly thereafter the
subpoena to appear in court September 17, at nine
o'clock. The days spent before the court date was filled
with much pain, tears, prayer, and praise, because, I
never doubted that God would not allow me to lose my
home. Arriving at the courthouse I noticed there was
very little activity, and once inside I learned there were
no cases scheduled that day due to it being the Jewish
New Year, Rosh Hashanah. What happened next was a
part of God's divine plan in teaching me what real
trusting Him meant. As I walked back to my car, I took
out my cell phone and noticed I had a missed call and as
I listened to the message I found that the dark alley I
had walked down had turned into a path by a flowing
gentle stream. The message simply said, "Ms. Byrd,

please call me, I have some good news." The good news

was my application was approved and the program

would pay all the arrears of the mortgage and would

make the monthly mortgage payments for the next year.

The caseworker told me with three strikes against me,

she honestly did not see any way possible for this to

have been approved. I kept telling her, "But, God", and

the fact that I trusted God because He assured me that

He had worked this out. My name is Queen K. Byrd and

this is my testimony of living Proverbs 3:5-6 at a time

when my faith seemed worn. I learned that my life was

set in order before I was born and that I was born on

purpose, with a purpose, to fulfill what God ordained for

my life. That measure of faith is all we need when we to

choose to trust in God.

~Queen~

I pray this testimony helps those who read it find

peace in the midst of their own storm. Persevering through

trials brings ultimate wholeness.

HAVE A BLESSED DAY!!!

Day 7 Study Questions

How has trusting God become the trademark of your

life?

_____

_____

_____

_____

_____

_____

_____

_____

_____

_____

_____

_____

_____

_____

How do you acknowledge God in all your ways?

_____

_____

_____

_____

_____

_____

_____

_____

_____

_____

_____

_____

_____

_____

How does this testimony help you recognize that

trusting God brings complete wholeness?

_____

_____

_____

_____

_____

_____

_____

_____

_____

_____

_____

_____

_____

_____

Day 8

Persevering Through Suffering Brings Wholeness

Psalm 19:34

"Many are the afflictions of the righteous, but the Lord delivers him out of them all. He guards all his bones; not one of them is broken".

This is a simple yet so profound promise from our God. Unlike the fluffy messages of blissful living that many try to shove down our throats, God promises that the believer will have many troubles. This Psalm was written when David was on the run for his life from Saul, believing he was going to kill him. The Greek word for suffering here is **pathema** which means to undergo and endure deep affliction. How ironic that the same God who promised in Joel 2:25 that He would *"restore what the locust have eaten"*; also promises suffering and trouble. In essence, although we will have to endure suffering we have the reassurance that God will also send deliverance, either in this life or the one to come.

As believers, we must conclude that believing in God and living righteously will not keep us from trouble, but will bring trying times and persecution, but the rewards come through perseverance. To enter the kingdom of God we must go through the narrow door of hardship, which is why many opt for the broad road leading to destruction. I have had the privilege over the years, as a result of my work with young people, to meet some amazing youth who are sold out for God. The testimony you are about to read comes from one of those awe-inspiring youth. I recall receiving a phone call from her mother in law that truly broke my heart. However, I knew that God had a plan even in the midst of the heartbreak that she would have to endure. Read her testimony and how she continues to tread that narrow road.

I will never forget that day. I was sitting in a CVS bathroom watching and waiting. The box said to wait three minutes, but I felt like I was waiting 3 hours! Finally, a very faint pink line appeared. According to the box, that meant I was pregnant. My heart was beating

out of my chest. "Me, pregnant," I thought to myself.

"I'm not ready, what about school; I need a job with

more money"! Thoughts rushed through my head like a

category five hurricane. It didn't take me long, however,

to forget the worrying and embrace the beautiful fact

that I was about to have a child.

That same day I told all my immediate family.

Everyone was excited and began preparing as if the

baby was going to be here the next day. I was only five

weeks pregnant when I found out. Weeks went by and it

was time to begin consistently going to the doctor's

office. Every time I went, I heard only good news.

"Strong heartbeat" my doctor would say, and I was

especially excited when I passed the 12 weeks mark. The

chances of a miscarriage were slim to none, so I felt

confident that this baby was definitely coming.

I was beginning to feel her move in me and that was the best part. If I was having a bad day that would always make me feel better. She was my new inspiration. I wanted to be and do better just for her. I felt myself pushing myself like never before because I wanted to be the best mom to this gift that God was giving me. I remember deciding on her name as well. My niece was in town and giving me suggestions. She said what about the name Jayla. As soon as she said that I fell in love. Jayla wasn't a different or unique name, but for whatever reason, that name felt right. I went to my husband about it and he agreed! We decided that she would have her dad's initials, Jayla Janelle Anderson. It was perfect and so was she!

February 11th, 2016 I was in my car in the driveway of my house and I prayed before walking in. "God, not my will but yours". February 12th, 2016 I was admitted in the hospital and Jayla went home to the Lord. I couldn't *believe it when the doctor told me. He said I was*

experiencing a spontaneous abortion (miscarriage)

"Why was this happening Lord"? I thought to myself.

"Why did she have to go"? "What was the point of her

being here in the first place"? I experienced so many

different emotions, had so many questions and still

struggle to this day.

I do not have the answers to all my questions and

there are still nights that I cry myself to sleep. However,

in the midst of my hurt, God has been my comfort.

Sometimes even my husband does not understand how I

feel, but I know God does. If you are going through

something similar to this, I encourage you to trust God.

Nobody can understand your hurt more that God.

TRUST HIM! And know that your pain can always

bring help and encouragement to someone else.

~Jayla Janelle Anderson~

February 12th, 2016

4 Months 2 Weeks

It is my prayer that this testimony from Jayla's mother brings hope and encouragement to your situation. Always know and believe that God does not go back on His promises. Though your afflictions may be many and at times overwhelming, He has promised to deliver you from them all. No matter how long you must wait for your deliverance, never give up on God, because persevering through suffering truly does bring wholeness.

HAVE A BLESSED DAY!!!

Day 8 Study Questions

How does the promise of afflictions and trials for the believer affect you?

_____

_____

_____

_____

_____

_____

_____

_____

_____

_____

_____

_____

_____

_____

How have you proven that persevering through trials

brings wholeness?

_____

_____

_____

_____

_____

_____

_____

_____

_____

_____

_____

_____

_____

_____

How does this testimony encourage you to persevere in crisis?

_____

_____

_____

_____

_____

_____

_____

_____

_____

_____

_____

_____

_____

_____

Day 9

A Lifestyle of Faith Brings Wholeness

Hebrews 11:6

"But without faith it is impossible to please Him, for he who comes to God must believe that He is and that He is a rewarder of those who diligently seek Him".

Faith **(peitho)** is a very strong word that believers sometimes tend to utilize on a whim. However, as I write this chapter I find myself in a position where I have to totally depend on God for every single thing, no matter how minute it may seem to others. Webster's dictionary defines faith as "allegiance to duty or a person; belief and trust in and loyalty to God; firm belief in something for which there is no proof; complete trust". I wish to focus today on the portion of the definition that speaks to exhibiting complete trust. This scripture implicitly states that we cannot bring pleasure to God if we do not have complete trust in Him.

"Blessed [with spiritual security] is the man who believes and trusts in and relies on the LORD *and whose hope and confident expectation is the* LORD. *For he will be [nourished] like a tree planted by the waters, that spreads out its roots by the river, and will not fear the heat when it comes; but its leaves will be green and moist. And it will not be anxious and concerned in a year of drought nor stop bearing fruit* (Jeremiah 17:7-8). No matter what we encounter in this journey of life God has promised to bless us, but the stipulation is that we trust Him. Complete trust is an awesome request because it is not in those tangible things that we can embrace, touch and experience, but the unseen things that we can only hope for. This scripture in Jeremiah comes off the heels of verses that declare curses for those who trust in men and depend on fleshly things for strength (5-6). Therefore, if the believer desires blessing he/she must trust God unreservedly. This complete and unwavering trust

is the only way, according to the writer in Hebrews, to truly
please God.

This morning I woke up in my new two bedroom
apartment in San Diego, after moving here two weeks
ago. I prayed and believed God that it was His will for
me to move in an effort to help my children and
grandchildren. This was the most difficult move of my
life. I rented out my four bedroom house, that God gave
me eight years ago, to complete strangers, sold most of
my belongings and moved to a small two bedroom
apartment in a big city that is completely foreign to me.
I depleted a lot of my savings to accomplish this feat,
believing and trusting that God would provide
everything I need. I remember sitting on the plane
wondering if I truly heard God or if this was a very big
mistake. Either way, there was no turning back because
I had forfeited just about everything I had to make this
come to pass.

As I look at my bank account getting smaller and smaller, I can feel the palpitations in my heart getting stronger and stronger each day. Yesterday was Sunday and I had been praying all week for God to lead me to a church that felt like home. I drove to one church that I was invited to and drove around in circles never actually finding this church. I leaned my head against the car window and asked God if I was really getting through to Him in my prayers, or if my prayers had become just an exercise in futility. I ventured back home and decided I would just watch church on TV. This did not feel right so I went online determined to find a church and the first one I saw was "New Creation Church". I did a brief research and ventured out to another unknown territory. As I walked into the sanctuary I felt a certain comfort as the ushers led me to my seat. A woman looked up at me with the most amazing inviting smile I had ever seen and I immediately felt connected somehow. I am not sure if this is the church I will call home, but I will definitely invest time in attending and believe God to reveal if this is where He would have me to attend and serve. When it was time to give tithes and offering yesterday I found myself contemplating holding back my tithes, because money was so short, however, I knew in doing that I would be robbing God, so I quickly wrote the check for my tithes.

Today I woke up in tears wondering again where the finances would be coming from to pay my bills. I reached out to my daughter and she asked a question; "do you believe this is where God wants you to be"? I had difficulty responding to the question because in that moment I honestly did not know. She immediately reminded me that my confidence in God had been shaken. She said it was only when I regained my confidence that I would be able to walk in the faith God is requiring in this season. She quoted Job 5:7-12 "For *man is born for trouble, [as naturally] as sparks fly*

upward. "As for me, I would seek God and inquire of

Him, and I would commit my cause to God; who does

great and unsearchable things, marvelous things without

number. "He gives rain upon the earth and sends waters

upon the fields so that He sets on high those who are

lowly, and He lifts to safety those who mourn. "He

frustrates the devices and schemes of the crafty so that

their hands cannot attain success or achieve anything of

[lasting] worth".

The tears ran down my face as she proceeded to

pray for me, declaring and decreeing that God would

show up for me just like He had always done. As she

exited the phone call I picked up a book I had been

reading called "Fervent" by bestselling author Priscilla

Shirer. I had reached the conclusion of this amazing

book about exhibiting fervent prayer and was reminded

by this powerful woman of God that my heavenly Father

is *"quietly working on my behalf without any fanfare; preparing, arranging and planning for my good" (p. 189). This was the jolt I needed today to reignite the fire in me to exercise a lifestyle of faith that will produce wholeness.*

~Sharon~

I pray for my sisters again today that this testimony will ignite something in you to completely trust God with your future. No matter what it seems like God has a plan and your circumstance is a part of it. Keep the faith and walk in wholeness.

HAVE A BLESSED DAY!!!

Day 9 Study Questions

How is your exhibition of faith pleasing God today?

_____

_____

_____

_____

_____

_____

_____

_____

_____

_____

_____

_____

_____

_____

_____

How are you practicing faith as a lifestyle?

_____

_____

_____

_____

_____

_____

_____

_____

_____

_____

_____

_____

_____

_____

_____

_____

How has today's devotion ignited in you a desire to completely trust God when you can't see Him?

_____

_____

_____

_____

_____

_____

_____

_____

_____

_____

_____

_____

_____

_____

_____

_____

Day 10

Living Water Brings Wholeness

John 4:13-14

*"Jesus answered her, "Everyone who drinks this water
will be thirsty again. But whoever drinks the water that I
give him will never be thirsty again. But the water that I
give him will become in him a spring of water [satisfying
his thirst for God] welling up [continually flowing,
bubbling within him] to eternal life".*

Research says the body is about 60% water and we are constantly losing water by means of urine and sweat. Therefore, health experts propose we drink eight 8 ounce glasses of water daily, to help replenish what we lose. I have tried over the years to get as close to consuming that amount as possible, yet I still find myself thirsty no matter how much I drink. Every time I read this scripture I can't help but wonder what this woman must have felt like in her encounter with the Christ concerning this living water He had to offer. One commentary declares "it is the inner never-failing source, the fountain of living water, which satisfies every want as it occurs". This is the awesome wellspring of life offered by our heavenly Father when we decide to truly acquaint ourselves with Him as Lord.

Amidst all the forbidding of His disciples, Jesus felt a dire need to go through Samaria, though Jews were not to acquaint themselves with Samaritans at that time. It was no coincidence that He met this estranged woman at a well because this was the significance of the water He was about to offer her. Jesus promised this sinful uninformed woman that if she chose the water He had to offer, it would spring up in her very soul and produce eternal life. The woman must have wondered; who is this crazy man, thinking He has what it takes to give me abundant life. She realized to herself that if He only knew who she was and the extremity of her waywardness He would never stop to speak to her, let alone make this offer. Yet, for some strange reason, she continued in this seemingly bizarre dialogue with a stranger she had never met.

This woman knew she had already exhibited a lifestyle that rendered her alienated in the sight of society. She had done what Jeremiah 2:13 reveals when it declares *"For My people have committed two evils: they have abandoned (rejected) me, the fountain of living water, and they have carved out their own cisterns, broken cisterns that cannot hold water".* Her lifestyle spoke to the fact that she had already carved out some broken cisterns for herself, and was considered hopeless. However, here stood a man explaining to her that there was hope and it rested in Him as the life-giving water that she needed to quench her thirst eternally. After this lengthy discourse and the revelation that He spoke to her, despite knowing who she was and the filthy existence she had chosen, she soon recognized this was no ordinary man, but the Lamb of God who has the power to remove sin. She then affirmed, *"Come, see a man, which told me all things that ever I did: is not this the Christ"* (vs. 29)? This is the beckoning we should all have when we realize the major sacrifice made for us to drink from this living water that leads to everlasting life. The following testimony is a testament of a present day meeting at the wellspring of life.

He must needs go through Samaria.

I cannot tell how many times I've been in love. It seems almost trivial how I would try by any means to love anyone, even if they did not want me to love them. Abuse was no stranger to me. I had known the hands of cousins, a stepfather, a step brother I had known the hands of suitors and men who I held so dearly.

It became normal at one point. Living life as an object as opposed to being a person. I had known no other love than the one my private parts could offer. So that was all I offered. Wrapped up in a negligee, love lingering on every wall, waiting to consume whoever would let it. Their love was nothing less than a convenience. I was convenient, I came with benefits.

Independent, I had my own, cooking, cleaning,

presentable at the drop of a dime. It just worked to call

me instead: "no strings they said." As the list of suitors

grew longer, I realized that there was a longing that

would not be appeased, a thirst that could not be

quenched. No matter how many men I had, fancy

restaurants I went to, private tours through another

country, soaking in the finer things in life; nothing filled

me. I only saw them, never me.

One day, after failing emotionally in most

departments, the Holy Spirit led me to a well. He

needed me to know that no amount of water would

make it better. I was cut down. I could not sprout. But

when I surrendered to the precious Lamb of God, his

living water began to fill my soul. Without any

reservations, He touched me. It wasn't like any other

touch I had ever known. It did not take. It only gave. I

understood then what it felt like to be pure; to be valued;

to be wanted; to be loved.

~Anna~

I pray this testimony reaches into the very core of your existence and reminds you how measureless the love of God truly is. When we reach into the recesses of our being, the realization is that we too like the woman at the well, after an encounter with the life-giving Savior, must say with enthusiasm "Come see a Man". It is the prayer of my heart that you recognize that Living Water truly does bring wholeness.

HAVE A BLESSED DAY!!!

Day 10 Study Question

How does the meeting at the well express the depth of

God's love for us?

_____

_____

_____

_____

_____

_____

_____

_____

_____

_____

_____

_____

_____

_____

_____

How have you been extending the salvation message to come see a Man?

_____

_____

_____

_____

_____

_____

_____

_____

_____

_____

_____

_____

_____

_____

How does the testimony for today remind you that

Living Water brings wholeness?

_____

_____

_____

_____

_____

_____

_____

_____

_____

_____

_____

_____

_____

_____

Day 11

Seasons of Testing Brings Wholeness

Psalm 46:1-3

"God is our refuge and strength [mighty and impenetrable], a very present and well-proved help in trouble. Therefore we will not fear, though the earth should change and though the mountains be shaken and slip into the heart of the seas, though its waters roar and foam, though the mountains tremble at its roaring".

We may experience emptiness at times, but God wants us to know He is our covering on every terrain and desires closeness with us. He is always there to comfort and help us. The psalmist expresses the fact that as believers, we must trust and be confident in God to provide security and stability, even when we feel barren and parched in our spirits. There will be times of doubt and difficulty, but we have been promised God's power to endure. Refuge (Greek = **machaseh**), is a picture of protection during times of danger, revealing that God is the security we need when life's storms overtake us. Strength (Greek = **dunamis**), reveals the power of God when we come up against the attacks of Satan and demonic forces. This strength equips us with energy to get through the stumbling blocks of life.

The outcome is the fact that God is *"a very present and well-proved help in trouble"*. He is always available to His children and grants us access to His throne room to call on Him all the time. He promises to *"NEVER [under any circumstances] DESERT YOU [nor give you up nor leave you without support, nor will He in any degree leave you helpless], NOR WILL HE FORSAKE or LET YOU DOWN or RELAX HIS HOLD ON YOU [assuredly not]"* (Hebrews 13:5)! Hence, we do not need to fear. In verse 3 the psalmist uses figurative expressions to symbolize the confusions and turmoil the world will face. In the midst of all this, God's people have no reason to fear. Through wars and rumors of wars that have been Biblically predicted, the believer must rest in the refuge of God.

*The figurative expression of mountains falling
into the sea became vividly clear recently when I
relocated for a season to San Diego to answer the call to
help my family. God strategically placed me in a
mountainous region of this city. As I walked outside the
first week, I looked up, and all I saw was a huge
mountain that seemed to surround me. People from all
walks of life were climbing up and down as though this
was a normal everyday activity, which as I have come to
realize actually is. I decided that memorable morning to
take that climb with no one around to help if I fall. As I
trudged up the mountain, which was a lot higher than I
thought, my life flashed before me and I realized I
needed to climb as high as I could to gain a better
understanding of my life challenges, that cause me to
stumble at times.*

*As I got to a strategic spot on that mountain I felt
myself slip and a woman next to me asked if I needed*

her help. I looked her square in the eyes and said I think I am going to make my way back down because this is a lot bigger than I thought. She looked back at me and declared, "Don't give up yet, Go a little bit further". It was as if God was talking to me about everything that was transpiring in my life. I looked down the mountain that morning as far as my eyes could see and thanked God for being the Creator (Elohim) that He is. I continued my journey a little further up and with every step I could hear God declaring "He is my refuge and strength, a very present help in times of trouble". I knew trouble was on the horizon, but I also felt I could trudge through it because God was going to help me. It has been almost three months since that memorable climb, and though I did not get all the way to the top and have not made the climb since, I am cognizant of the fact that God will always be my refuge and strength.

~Sharon~

I am not sure what you are facing on your uphill journey today my sisters, but I do know that God is going to equip you with all you need at this juncture of your journey. Though you may face a season of emptiness, and you may even stumble and fall, God is with you and will guide you through those slippery crevices that seem impassable at times. Hold fast to your God and allow Him to be what He promised to be "your refuge and strength" in times of trouble.

HAVE A BLESSED DAY!!!

Day 11 Study Questions

How does knowing that God is your protector get you through seasons of testing?

_____

_____

_____

_____

_____

_____

_____

_____

_____

_____

_____

_____

_____

_____

_____

When you experience seasons of testing, how does

knowing God is your refuge encourage you?

_____

_____

_____

_____

_____

_____

_____

_____

_____

_____

_____

_____

_____

_____

What mountains must you overcome to get to your next season?

_____

_____

_____

_____

_____

_____

_____

_____

_____

_____

_____

_____

_____

_____

_____

_____

Day 12

Sufficiency of Grace Brings Wholeness

2 Corinthians 12:7-9

Because of the surpassing greatness and extraordinary nature of the revelations [which I received from God], for this reason, to keep me from thinking of myself as important, a thorn in the flesh was given to me, a messenger of Satan, to torment and harass me—to keep me from exalting myself! Concerning this I pleaded with the Lord three times that it might leave me; but He has said to me, "My grace is sufficient for you [My loving kindness and My mercy are more than enough—always available—regardless of the situation]; for [My] power is being perfected [and is completed and shows itself most effectively] in [your]weakness." Therefore, I will all the more gladly boast in my weaknesses, so that the power of Christ [may completely enfold me and] may dwell in me.

Paul the apostle explains in this scripture an incessant thorn that has been allotted to him by God to keep him humble. The word thorn is indicative of pain, difficulty, affliction, shame or some kind of physical illness. There is no exact significance given for this uncomfortable prickle in his flesh, but we are told that part of the reasoning behind it was to keep this great apostle from thinking too highly of himself. It was obvious

that Paul was in constant prayer about the infliction, as it

brought great discomfort. Though it seemed to be causing

great pain to the point of torment, the apostle was very

unclear as to what it really was. Therefore, there are a variety

of speculations among Biblical scholars as to what it could be.

The Greek word used here for thorn is **skolop**, meaning

thorn or stake. When we think of the word stake it conjures

up thoughts of something sharp, that when used, causes

excruciating pain. I recall being younger and watching

vampire movies with my friends and a stake was always the

one thing that could be used to finally terminate the life of

the vampire. In ancient times this instrument was used as a

form of torture. Thus, it is obvious that whatever it was, it

was meant to bring hurt, and was causing an unceasing illness

in Paul's body.

This thorn in the flesh that Paul speaks of was said to

be, a courier of Satan which he meant for evil; but God

intended it, and overrode it for good. How marvelous to

know that even the most painful of circumstances in our

lives, though intended by Satan to kill us, can be used by our

heavenly Father to bring us good. Prayer is a soothing

measure used to counteract every sore, it is a medicine for all

maladies of life; and when we are beset with thorns in the

flesh, we must immerse ourselves in prayer. Dilemmas are

sent to bring us to our knees, and they sometimes persist to

teach us to remain instant in prayer. After Paul prayed three

times for this malady to leave him, God uttered these all-

consuming words ***"My grace is sufficient for you"***. How

awesome to know; that no matter how painful our

circumstance that God's grace is all sufficient for what ails us.

He remains El Shaddai our all-sufficient One who cares for

us and knows what's best for us all the time. As I write to

encourage my sisters on this day, I have chosen to share a

testimony from my niece about a time when there was a

thorn in her flesh, and how it taught her to truly trust in God.

Recently I have had some personal let downs and was faced with a decision. Do I continue trusting in God's promises and believe even when I cannot see my way through, or do I fold up, call it quits and give up. It was very tempting to give in to thoughts of fear, disappointment, and defeat, but then I was reminded that Hope is the anchor for my soul and my Hope is in God. Not my situation, not in a person, but in God alone.

I have a habit I started a few years ago where I begin thinking back on God's faithfulness and what He has brought me through. I then remembered the most trying time of faith in my life. It was about 15 years ago. I was in my early twenties and full of life and energy. I was always a very active young lady, working out, eating healthy, and very health conscious overall. Slowly, though, my energy started to drain. Every day I felt like I could not keep my eyes open, I was always cold, I was also breathless. Then my symptoms got worse. Going up the stairs felt like I was climbing a mountain, and I would start to sweat as if I had just finished a 45-minute cardio workout.

It all came crashing down one day while at work. I felt so sick and dizzy that I asked to leave work early. As I was pulling out, I was so disoriented I hit a co-worker's car in the parking lot. This is when I said to myself, "Almarie you have a serious issue", and got myself to the doctor. My co-worker was kind enough to see I was not well and let me go to the doctor and deal with the insurance issue later.

This doctor visit changed my life forever. The doctor sent me for blood work and sent me home to rest. They called me the very next day and said Ms. Marshall; I have an appointment set up for you at the hospital. You need a blood transfusion right away! I was shocked and confused. I told my parents with whom I was still living at the time, and we all went to the hospital. My

doctor was there as well. I was admitted immediately

into the ICU and set up for the transfusion, but also

another battery of tests. The blood transfusion went

well, and immediately I felt warm for the first time in

over a year! The doctors were still very concerned

because my test results showed that my blood count was

still mysteriously low, but my blood iron count was

normal.

I was sent to specialist after specialist until I was

sent to a Hematologist. It was then that I was diagnosed

with A-plastic Anemia, a very rare blood disorder. It was

also determined that my bone marrow stopped working.

This was very dangerous. It meant I did not have

enough blood cells to fight off any infections. I was then

told I would need a bone marrow transplant or I could

possibly die. The doctors were all very concerned and

spoke in hushed tones regarding my case. I was referred

to Jackson Memorial Hospital. At this point I started

feeling sick again, lethargic, and every bone in my body

ached. I was told if I got sick or got an infection it would

be very dangerous for me.

My parents started praying unceasingly for me.

Elders, pastors, and my friends all prayed for me. They

were all scared for me, more than I was for myself. My

father called an impromptu prayer meeting the night

before I was to go to the Jackson Memorial Hospital. He

called us all to gather in the living room and form a

circle. As we held hands he simply prayed, "Lord Jesus,

we need a miracle and we know you are more than able

to heal my daughter. Release your power into her very

marrow and re-charge her". At that instant, I felt a bolt

of electricity course through me starting in my hands

and like a shock wave across my chest and out to the

other hand. I literally cried out in pain and asked: "who

shocked me". Everyone just started staring at me in an

odd silent way. I felt warm and revived! I started running

all over my house shouting" I am healed"!! "I know I

am healed"!

The next day I was prepped for a blood panel and

then another blood test before going through with the

bone marrow matching process to see if my sister was a

match, or if I would need a donor. Before they could do

anything they had to get my blood results. When my

results came back 6 doctors and their 6 assistants and

medical students came into my room. I thought, "Oh

no, this can't be good". The head doctors said, "Well it

seems there must have been an error in your previous

tests because your bone marrow biopsy results just came

back, and your bone marrow is working". The only

explanation they had was that all the other 3-4 tests done

previously were wrong. I looked the doctor right in the

eyes and told him, "well my dad prayed for me last night

and I know it's a miracle". He chuckled as did all the

other doctors and students, and said "That is impossible", but they all still had an awestruck, baffled look on their faces. I smiled my own knowing smile because I knew the truth. What took place in my body only God could do. I said, "Thank you for the good news doctor", and walked out of the hospital that day knowing I was healed. Yes, I would still face battles in the years to come and have more transfusions, but no longer did I need a transplant. My healing has been a progression of getting better and stronger year after year. I have learned God's miracle work is final, but the proof of complete healing can come all at once, or progressively. In my case, The Lord has done a sudden all at once thing, and also a slow progressive healing. What He does is yes, and Amen! A final work; that must manifest here on earth, in an earthly time frame.

Recently I went to the doctor and my blood count is higher than it has ever been and is in the normal range

for the first time in 15 years! In retrospect, I can see
God's faithfulness and goodness. No matter what I face
today, He is continuing to do more than I can ever ask,
imagine, or think. So I choose to believe that
NOTHING is impossible with God. "Be healed and Be
whole". In Jesus' name,

~Almarie~

It is my hope that whatever you are going through today and no matter how painful it may be that this scripture, culminated with the testimony, has helped you to embrace God as El Shaddai (all sufficient). Pray to the God of all comfort and know that His strength is perfected when you are at your weakest. I encourage you to eat from this word today and recognize that the all-sufficiency of God truly does bring wholeness.

HAVE A BLESSED DAY!!!

Day 12 Study Questions

What is a thorn that you have been living with?

_____

_____

_____

_____

_____

_____

_____

_____

_____

_____

_____

_____

_____

_____

How has the thorn affected your relationship with God?

_____

_____

_____

_____

_____

_____

_____

_____

_____

_____

_____

_____

_____

_____

_____

_____

How has God proved that His grace is sufficient in the

midst of your situation?

_____

_____

_____

_____

_____

_____

_____

_____

_____

_____

_____

_____

_____

_____

Day 13

Welcoming Victory Brings Wholeness

Isaiah 54:17

*"No weapon that is formed against you will succeed;
And every tongue that rises against you in judgment you
will condemn. This [peace, righteousness, security, and
triumph over opposition] is the heritage of the servants
of the LORD,
And this is their vindication from Me," says the LORD.*

We often hear this verse repeated over and over when we are going through times of adversity. It is either

reiterated by friends or loved ones, who mean us well, or it

bombards our minds till we almost want to say STOP! God

originally gave this scripture to the prophet Isaiah in an effort

to bring comfort to Israel in a season of distress. He allowed

him to use this imagery of a great future for Israel, even

though at the time God's chosen people were experiencing a

time when it looked like God had abandoned them. In a few

verses prior to this one the prophet declared to the people

"Do not fear, for you will not be put to shame, And do

not feel humiliated or ashamed, for you will not be

disgraced. For you will forget the shame of your youth"

(Isaiah 54:4). The people were given the assurance that even

though they had to suffer, God would remain their

Redeemer. The chapter has constant reminders of who God

was and continued to be for His chosen people. God used

the prophet to enlighten them that no matter what it felt like,

and even when everything around them was crumbling they

should remember that His covenant with them would not be

broken. In another portion of this chapter God encourages

His children by declaring: *"O you afflicted [city], storm-*

tossed, and not comforted, Listen carefully, I will set

your [precious] stones in mortar, And lay your

foundations with sapphires. "And I will make your

battlements of rubies, And your gates of [shining] beryl

stones, And all your [barrier] walls of precious stones

(Isaiah 54:11-12). He needed to instill in them exactly who He

was and the fact that no matter what it looked like or felt like,

His covering was greater than any weapon that would come against them.

This same comfort is meant for us as believers who face affliction and turmoil as we go through the seasons of life. When the storms of life's circumstances weigh us down we have to remember that the things that come against us to destroy us will not prevail. In Isaiah 54:16 God assures us *"Listen carefully, I have created the smith who blows on the fire of coals And who produces a weapon for its purpose, And I have created the destroyer to inflict ruin.* He comes behind that in verse 17 to remind us that it is these conditions that cause Him to have compassion on us, put His loving arms around us and impart the spiritual strength that it will require to go through the testing and come forth unscathed. My daughter Shanae has had many circumstances that have literally come upon her to kill her and destroy the ministry that God has birthed in her. She writes:

*"There is going to be a shift". Words told to me
by a prophetess. In that moment I didn't understand it.
This phrase, to most, is simple; God is going to shift
some things. In my mind all I could think was, God, I
can't bear to go through anything else. Less than a week
later the shift began. I felt like God had literally kicked
me out of my comfort zone and into a place of darkness
and complete misery. I woke up day after day with what
felt like a brick on my chest. The thought of getting up
and surviving yet another day seemed impossible. I felt
that as the days went by the further I got from God. The
constant thoughts of "God did I miss you"? Flooded my
brain and pain became reality. I walked daily in fear of
the unknown.*

*Suddenly I was reminded; God has not given me
a spirit of fear, but of power, love, and a sound mind".
This promise began to bring me life, it began to bring
peace to my, what seemed impossible, circumstances.*

As the days progressed, my problems became irrelevant, as I recovered my strength. Rather than focusing on the chaos that surrounded me, I focused on my relationship with my Father. My pastor stated one Sunday that "knowing Him is my power". I serve a God who can and will make the impossible possible. I kept myself in constant worship, I studied my Word and my spirit man grew stronger and stronger. I finally understood who I was in Him. My name was no longer pain, insecurity, sadness, anger or fear. My name is now peace, joy, security, intercessor, warrior; unconquerable force to be reckoned with. With every step, every journey, I draw closer to my Father. He calls me Victory and no matter the circumstances "No weapon forged against me will prosper. I have been shifted.

~Victory~

~Shanae~

Though it is not stated exactly what the circumstances were that surrounded Shanae, seeking to tear her down, it is obvious the enemy wanted to use any and everything going on in her life at that time to render her feeble and useless. However, when she embraced the shift instead of running away from it, she was reminded that *"no weapon formed against her would prosper"* and God was changing her name to Victory. May this scripture and testimony remind you today that in the midst of your circumstances, God's plan is to make you a victor and not a victim.

HAVE A BLESSED DAY!!!

Day 13 Study Questions

How can you utilize the weapons that come your way to

bring God glory?

_____

_____

_____

_____

_____

_____

_____

_____

_____

_____

_____

_____

_____

When the storms of life rage, how can you declare

victory over your circumstances?

_____

_____

_____

_____

_____

_____

_____

_____

_____

_____

_____

_____

_____

_____

_____

How is knowing that God is going to lay your

foundations with sapphires help you in your journey to

His expected end?

_____

_____

_____

_____

_____

_____

_____

_____

_____

_____

_____

_____

_____

_____

Day 14

Complete Forgiveness Brings Wholeness

Matthew 6:14-15

*For if you forgive others their trespasses [their reckless
and willful sins], your heavenly Father will also forgive
you. But if you do not forgive others [nurturing your
hurt and anger with the result that it interferes with your
relationship with God], then your Father will not forgive
your trespasses.*

As believers, forgiveness always seems to be the most difficult task, especially when it pertains to matters of the heart. The scripture above clearly specifies what forgiveness entails in God's economy. Prior to these verses about what is required as it pertains to forgiveness, Jesus first teaches His disciples and us to pay close attention as to the how and why of performing acts of kindness or charity. The question is asked: "are we doing service to please men or to please God"? The only services that will be rewarded in heaven are those performed in an effort to bring God pleasure. Those who render acts of service to be seen are referred to as hypocrites, acting under a mask and not genuine. Acts of service must be done in secret, so God can reward us openly. He then goes on to give us a recipe for prayer:

1. Enter our secret closet and close the door – the secrecy of prayer.

2. Don't use vain repetition – the uncomplicated, directness of prayer.

3. Reverence the Father – the awe of prayer.

4. Thy Kingdom come – petition for the second return.

5. Thy will be done - petitioning the will of God in heaven and on earth.

Subsequent to that formula for prayer, He culminates by commanding us to forgive others, in the same way, He forgives us; which is directly followed by us requesting to be delivered from evil. It is here that we are given the exhortation of verses 14-15. This prescription for forgiveness cannot be taken lightly because it is only as we forgive that God is given the impetus to forgive us.

When I consider all that God has forgiven me for over the years, it brings me to a place of reconciling with the fact that I must forgive those who have sought to hurt and harm me, whether willingly or not. There is no hurt or harm that I have encountered that can compare to the hurt I brought upon my heavenly Father when I turned my back on Him on so many different occasions. I wallowed in the dirt with the pigs of the world, to the point of looking and smelling like them. Yet when I came to the end of my worldly exploits, put my tail between my legs and went back to my Father, He stretched out His arms, embraced me and gave a celebratory party upon my return. What a mighty God we serve, who, in spite of our many indiscretions, forgives and loves us with an everlasting love.

It was the night of Monday, April 6, 2015, as I waited up for my husband, as I had recently grown accustomed to doing as I watched him slip back into his old lifestyle. Prior to our marriage in 2010, he walked me through a park, explaining the pitfalls of his journey to that point. His journey had taken him through a drug habit and a six-year prison sentence which he said brought him freedom behind bars. Our marriage had almost spanned five years and here I was waiting upon this most fateful night of our marriage. The hours grew longer and longer and my heart was racing out of my chest. I had always told my husband that if he reverted to his old ways that would be the one thing I could not forgive or live with. It was now 3:00 am as I lay flat on my back looking up at the ceiling wondering where he was. I heard the fateful ping on my phone as it lit up with a text message I will never forget. All it said was "please help me I relapsed". There were no messages for two and a half days after that and all I kept thinking was he would be found dead somewhere.

With the help of faithful friends, I drove for hours and finally found my husband, strung out on crack cocaine. My most fateful nightmare had come true and as I watched him fall out of the truck and onto the pavement begging my forgiveness, all I felt was pain and hurt that was indescribable. He ended up in the emergency room that night and a lot transpired since then, but through it all, God has taught me that complete forgiveness brings wholeness. Though the turmoil of this saga continues, I learn daily to forgive him and others who have brought me pain. More than that, I embrace the fact of 1 Corinthians 13:6 "love holds no record of wrongs".

~Sharon~

As you read this testimony and the scripture, I pray that you will recognize the importance of forgiving those who have brought you pain and hurt. Remember my sisters how much God has forgiven you for and set yourself and those who hurt you free. There is an unexplainable sense of

freedom and wholeness that exudes when finally you learn to

say from the very core of your being "I forgive you". I pray

on this day that you find healing and wholeness by forgiving.

HAVE A BLESSED DAY!!!

Day 14 Study Questions

How do you forgive even when the person causing you

pain is not sorry?

_____

_____

_____

_____

_____

_____

_____

_____

_____

_____

_____

_____

What are the benefits of complete forgiveness?

_____

_____

_____

_____

_____

_____

_____

_____

_____

_____

_____

_____

_____

_____

_____

How will you confront the person/people you need to

forgive today?

_____

_____

_____

_____

_____

_____

_____

_____

_____

_____

_____

_____

_____

Day 15

Total Deliverance Brings Wholeness

Jeremiah 30:17

*"For I will restore health to you And I will heal your wounds, says the LORD, Because they have called you an outcast, saying:
This is Zion; no one seeks her and no one cares for her."*

This profound scripture speaks to the deliverance and restoration of Israel. Although the prisoners were justly enduring suffering, and seemingly helpless, the Lord planned to become visible for them and discipline their taskmasters; and He will still do so for His people today. Sometimes we may fall and discard our belief in God in an effort to do things simply because it feels good. The bottom line is we are in a backslidden state and in need of complete deliverance. We, at times, resort to healing ourselves, which in the long run becomes an exercise in futility. All attempts to heal ourselves prove unproductive, as long as we abandon our heavenly Advocate and His

vindicating Spirit.

God knows our hearts and thoughts and He is

waiting in those seasons of disobedience and He waits

patiently for us to seek deliverance. He wants to bring us

back to a comfortable and prosperous place. His desire is to

restore us back to Him and heal all our wounds. Sometimes

He has to orchestrate certain things in our lives to get our

undivided attention, thus, opening the door for deliverance.

God promised, through the prophet Jeremiah in verses 15-16:

"Why do you cry out over your injury [since it is the

natural result of your sin]? Your pain is incurable

(deadly). Because your guilt is great

and your sins are glaring and innumerable, I have done

these things to you. Therefore, all who devour you will

be devoured; and all your adversaries, every one of them,

will go into captivity. And they who plunder you will

become plunder, and all who prey upon you I will give

for prey." In essence, even though we walk away from God
and put ourselves in harm's way, He is waiting with open
arms to embrace us if we would only confess and be
delivered. Most times we are reluctant to return to Him
because we feel a major sense of guilt.

*I recall many years ago as a teenager, walking
away from God. I reveled so much in the world I became
a part of it and felt in my spirit there was no way God
could forgive me so I might as well continue. I spiraled
out of control daily without anyone around me
recognizing. I became a recluse and still called myself a
Christian. I went to so many house parties and clubs on
Fridays and Saturdays and still found myself in church
on Sundays, believing that would keep me holy. I knew
the Biblical language because most of my life was spent
in church memorizing verses, and sometimes entire
chapters. Those who thought they knew me accepted
me as one truly walking with the Lord. I managed to*

keep up the charade for years until God orchestrated a

plan that would get my undivided attention.

I have testified about this before and even wrote

about it in a book, but I don't think some really think

that God actually works in people's lives in the way I

have described. Some even say the way I was living was

not all that bad because all I was doing is having a good

time and not really hurting anyone. However, this

lifestyle came on the heels of me aborting a child and

seeking to cover the guilt with what I referred to as

good, clean fun. I knew deep in my spirit that there was

nothing good or clean about what I was doing and I was

literally dying inside. I believe God made a way to get

my attention, so He could deliver me from self-

destruction.

Just as the Israelites did in the scriptures above, I

was crying out in distress even though it was self-

inflicted. I looked amazingly beautiful on the outside in

those days but when I looked in the mirror all I saw was

ugly. God rescued me one fateful New Year's Eve night

when I was thrown from a moving car. In all honesty, I

think I faced death that night, but when I opened my

eyes I was very much alive with not even one scratch on

my body. God had delivered me from death and I owed

Him the rest of my life. I vowed while sitting on the

sidewalk that night that I would relinquish my crazy

lifestyle and walk with Him forever.

Over the years, up until 2013 when I wrote

"Weapons for Victory", though I knew God delivered

me, I found it difficult to tell anyone about my secret

life. I held on to my testimony, desiring to fit in with the

church folks all around me. It wasn't until I wrote the

book, over thirty years later, that I felt complete

deliverance from that season in my life. In Jeremiah

30:17, Zion represents a place of dryness. It wasn't until I wrote the book that I was able to say I no longer feel like I am in a place of dryness.

~Sharon~

I don't know where you are in your journey towards wholeness, but God has a place of wellness for you. Maybe you are experiencing a place of dryness and even thinking about giving up on God. Maybe God has delivered you from a horrific place in your life and like me, you fear testifying for fear of the masses. I encourage you today my dear sisters to experience the delivering power of God as you testify of His goodness, thus, being able to walk in true wholeness.

HAVE A BLESSED DAY!!!

Day 15 Study Questions

What does deliverance mean to you?

_____

_____

_____

_____

_____

_____

_____

_____

_____

_____

_____

_____

_____

_____

What has happened in your life that you still need

deliverance from?

_____

_____

_____

_____

_____

_____

_____

_____

_____

_____

_____

_____

_____

_____

How have the people around you hindered you from

experiencing real deliverance?

_____

_____

_____

_____

_____

_____

_____

_____

_____

_____

_____

_____

_____

_____

Day 16

Overcoming Adversity Brings Wholeness

Revelation 12:11

*And they overcame and conquered him because of the
blood of the Lamb and because of the word of their
testimony, for they did not love their life and renounce
their faith even when faced with death.*

The efforts of Satan were unproductive against the church and lethal to him. The warfare was in heaven; in Christ's church and God's kingdom here on earth. Those involved in this war are Christ, His followers, and Satan. Our strength in this great conflict is in having God in the frontline, advocating for our cause. When we get hit with adversity and God gives us the courage to withstand, our response in the battle is to testify, thus revealing to Satan we overcome by the word of our testimony.

Sometimes we find it difficult to testify about the amazing things God has done in our lives because we are afraid of what people may think, or how we will be perceived. Believers, however, have been admonished to faithfully testify so they can overcome and become whole. Satan wants God's people to shrivel up and die, especially after they have experienced dreadful things. When trials hit, the first thing we usually want to do is run and hide. However, God always has a plan to utilize our experiences to bring us good and bring Him glory. We bring him glory when we throw caution to the wind and set out to overcome, using those defining moments in our lives.

You're an Overcomer!!

To look at me, I appeared to have it all together. I attended church on a regular basis with my family. I have been married to the same person for 24 years. I have a remarkable 17 year old son. I am a teacher at a private Christian school in which I was named Teacher of the Year in 2015. Sure, we struggle a little financially, but who doesn't these days? All in all my life does not appear to be that bad; however, outward appearances can sometimes paint a picture that is not a true reflection of the inner person. In other words, people do not see the real you. People only see the person you want them to see.

So, who is the person that I was trying to hide? Who is this person that I did not want others to know about? I've kept this person a secret for so long that I've almost forgotten who she was. I was physically and emotionally abused as a child. I tried to do things "perfectly" in hopes the abuse would stop, which only led to obsessive compulsive tendencies as an adult. I was raped twice by two different men on two separate occasions. During this time, my 12 year old sister had also passed away. She was my world!! Did I mention that I blamed myself for her death? I had just turned 19.

To be honest with you, I thought your first experience with sex was supposed to be meaningful and *special, not forced, meaningless and so full of hate.*

Even though these events happened years ago, they

have had an enormous impact on my life as an adult.

Imagine being intimate with your husband and seeing

the men that raped you instead. Kind of ruins the

moment, don't you think? While my husband is

sympathetic of what happened to me, he constantly

reminds me that it is not fair for me to punish him for

something someone else did to me. That makes perfect

sense! He did not rape me, so why was I acting like he

was the one that did?

28 years is a long time to punish yourself for

things that happened so long ago, but I managed to pull

it off. Most people never knew about the inner struggles

that I dealt with on a daily basis, though. I knew that if I

was ever going to break free from these issues that have

plagued me, I was going to need some professional help

to do it. Because of all of the years that have gone by

and the severity of the situation, I knew that my situation was not going to have a "quick fix" solution. As I was going through counseling, I found that forgiving others was the easy part; forgiving myself was the part I struggled with the most. Forgiveness allows us to release the prisoner we've held deep inside. In order for us to be whole, we MUST be able to forgive those that have wronged us and to forgive ourselves.

As Christians, we all sin and have to come to the Father and repent for the sins we have committed. The Father will forgive us if we ask, so who are we to not forgive others who sin against us? The Bible tells us that God will not forgive us if we do not forgive others (Matthew 6:15). Forgiving others also means forgiving yourself! Ouch...that hurts!!!

Remember...You are not alone...You're an overcomer...You got this!!! You and God!!!

~Tracey~

The testimony of a woman wounded and scarred by the insurmountable trials of life, when shared with the masses allows her to overcome. Though you may be wrestling with circumstances that seem unbearable, God is exhorting you today to let go and let Him fix it. However, after the fixing, He requires something even more intense; that you tell the story so others can be fixed. This is the opportunity to overcome by the word of your testimony and experience wholeness.

HAVE A BLESSED DAY!!!

Day 16 Study Questions

What are some testimonies that you need to share so you can overcome?

_____

_____

_____

_____

_____

_____

_____

_____

_____

_____

_____

_____

_____

How will sharing your testimony make you experience

wholeness?

_____

_____

_____

_____

_____

_____

_____

_____

_____

_____

_____

_____

_____

How does knowing that God has your back make you

respond in seasons of adversities?

_____

_____

_____

_____

_____

_____

_____

_____

_____

_____

_____

_____

_____

_____

Day 17

Power from the Holy Spirit Brings Wholeness

Acts 1:8

But you will receive power and ability when the Holy Spirit comes upon you; and you will be My witnesses [to tell people about Me] both in Jerusalem and in all Judea, and Samaria, and even to the ends of the earth."

The most important purpose for the baptism in the Holy Spirit is to receive power. This power, in the Greek, is referred to as **dunamis** which is a mighty, miraculous power that is offered to all believers if they would just ask. It is not just a matter of speaking in other tongues, but being able to witness so that others could come to know Jesus as Savior and Lord. This power is more than strength and ability, but it is power in action to drive out demons and anoint the sick to be healed in the name of Jesus. The baptism in the Holy Spirit is for all who confess salvation, are born again and have received the indwelling of the Holy Spirit.

In the book of Acts, speaking in other tongues as the Spirit gives utterance is the primary external sign accompanying the baptism in the Holy Spirit. Jesus' key role in walking the earth was for His disciples to be baptized in the Holy Spirit and "clothed with power from on high". Acts 1:4-5 states: *"He commanded them not to leave Jerusalem, but to wait for what the Father had promised, "Of which," He said, "You have heard Me speak. For John baptized with water, but you will be baptized and empowered and united with the Holy Spirit, not long from now."* This is a specific gift of empowerment that He wants to bestow on all His children and all we have to do is ask. There is only one baptism in the Spirit experience, but there are new fillings offered to the believer after the initial baptism. We must constantly seek renewal and maintain our relationship with the Spirit.

Sometimes, as believers, we receive the baptism in the Holy Spirit and the circumstances of life hit and we abandon the power that has been bestowed on us. However, we are reminded here that we will receive dunamis power to witness to the nations. We will be able to lay hands on people and watch them be healed in Jesus name. We will cast out demons in Jesus name. With all this power in our hands, how do we just stand by and allow the enemy to wreak havoc in our homes, family, jobs and even our churches. Though this power is available to us, it is up to us to ask for it and when we receive it we must act upon it by using it.

I recall as a young adult wondering what it all meant to be baptized in the Holy Spirit. I grew up in a Plymouth brethren church where we were taught that when you got saved you were filled with the Holy Spirit and that's all there was to it. Therefore, when I ventured out of that denomination in 1987 and found God leading me to the Pentecostal regime, I was faced with culture shock, especially as it pertained to the Holy Spirit and the power that was at my disposal. There were Friday nights when I would attend the youth service and there would be teaching on being baptized in the Holy Spirit. When the altar call was made to receive this infilling I stayed in my seat because I felt I was already saved and that's all there was to it. I felt no need for empowerment because all was well with my life. I had already rededicated my life to the Lord, I was reading and praying religiously and all was well with me and God. I felt all this power was only for those in leadership of the church, or aspiring to be leaders. Since none of that applied to me, I would watch as these teachings were offered, as young people came to the altar, fell out on the floor and spoke in tongues that were unknown. I was positive that they were probably faking.

I decided to test the waters one Friday night after one of these teachings about the power of the Holy Spirit and being baptized in the Spirit. I went to the altar and I remember someone putting their hand on my forehead but nothing happened. When the altar call ended I was left standing while others around me were either on the floor or weeping or just bent over the altar. Though I had no reaction that night I was pricked in my spirit that there was something missing in my walk with the Lord. Though I had reconnected with Him, there was a power being offered that I had not received and to be honest it was scary. Whenever those teachings were offered in the future I found myself being more attuned to listening and learning about this baptism that everyone so desperately seemed to desire.

Years went by and I learned more and more about the power of the Holy Spirit and His ability to transform me and equip me with supernatural power. I was growing in leaps and bounds in my spiritual walk with God but I never received that gift of speaking in tongues. In 1991, after being married for only two years to my first husband, we were asked by the missions

*department if we would be willing to uproot our lives
and go to South Africa to facilitate a school that the
church was planting. While my husband at the time was
elated to go as a result of his long-standing work in
missions to people on the streets and subways, I was a
bit reluctant. I went to God on my face and told Him
how afraid I was to leave the comfort of home and
family to start over in a strange land. I prayed for about a
week on my face and God gave me peace about going.*

*A few days after making the decision to leave I
recall reading an interview with Cookie Johnson (wife of
Magic) in the essence magazine. He had recently
publicly disclosed the fact that he was HIV positive. I
read that magazine over and over, wondering what I
would do if I received that news. At the end of that
week, my former husband came into the house and told
me we were no longer able to go the South Africa
because he too was HIV positive. It is hard to explain*

what I felt in that moment, but after exhibiting all the

emotions I went on my face to pray. This time it was

different, though I was praying for healing for my

spouse I was praying for more power to come over me. I

knew it would take a supernatural power to fight this

war and win.

A visiting pastor from Pittsburgh came to our

church a few months later and during the altar call, she

beckoned us to come forward. She put the microphone

down and began ministering to us as if we were the only

ones in the room. She invited us to Pittsburgh for a time

of refreshing, paid for our hotel stay and treated us like

royalty. While in the church basement with her on the

Saturday of our stay, she spent some time ministering to

me. In the midst of her praying and anointing me with

oil, I felt a move of the Spirit like I never had before. I

realized this was the baptism in the Spirit that I was

missing. It was not just as a result of the manifestation

of speaking in tongues, but I felt a power come over me that I had never felt before. As I look back over my life 25 years later I realize that if it had not been for the supernatural power bestowed on me through the baptism in the Holy Spirit, I would not have made it through the storms of life I have had to face. Power from the Holy Spirit does bring complete wholeness.

~Sharon~

It is my hope that as you read this testimony if you have not experienced this supernatural move of the Spirit, you will ask God to baptize you and make you whole.

HAVE A BLESSED DAY!!!

Day 17 Study Questions

How does knowing you have access to supernatural

power make you live your life differently?

_____

_____

_____

_____

_____

_____

_____

_____

_____

_____

_____

_____

_____

_____

How can you embrace the dunamis power being offered

to you right now?

_____

_____

_____

_____

_____

_____

_____

_____

_____

_____

_____

_____

_____

_____

How will this power make a difference in the way you

approach the circumstances of life?

_____

_____

_____

_____

_____

_____

_____

_____

_____

_____

_____

_____

_____

_____

Day 18

Abandoning Temptations Brings Wholeness

1 Corinthians 10:13

*"No temptation [regardless of its source] has
overtaken or enticed you that is not common to human
experience [nor is any temptation unusual or beyond
human resistance]; but God is faithful [to His word—He
is compassionate and trustworthy], and He will not let
you be tempted beyond your ability [to resist], but along
with the temptation He [has in the past and is now and]
will [always] provide the way out as well, so that you will
be able to endure it [without yielding, and will overcome
temptation with joy]"*

Temptation has been the root of most of what ails us because we have not chosen the way of escape God promised and does provide. When I moved to San Diego recently, I was desperately searching for a church that felt like a good fit. Though I still don't know where that good fit is I have visited a few churches and met an abundance of wonderful people. I don't believe any of the people I have met have been by accident, but a part of God's strategic plan to either use them to bless me or use me to bless them. One of those people was my new friend and dear sister, Faye Malone. I met her one Sunday morning when she was getting in her car. All I saw was her fierce hair cut, which prompted me to say hello. We have connected in many ways since then, and after listening to her testimony, I thought it would change lives and should be read by many.

"Amazing Grace"; "Precious Lord, Take My Hand"; "I Don't Feel No Ways Tired"; to name a few, are some of the old gospel songs that have carried me these past eight and a half years. You see, eight and a half years ago, I had a medical procedure done on my brain; and during that process, my brain bled. I laid in an induced coma for several days. I never thought to ask the reason this was happening to me, as I laid in that bed immobile. I did not realize that I could not walk or use my left arm until I was fully awake from the coma. What was I going to ask God? I was angry with God!

I am a recovering addict and had been without the use of any mind, or mood altering substance in my veins since 1995. For fourteen years, I used to live and lived to use. I had many overdoses and spent several stays in local jails. During those tumultuous years, as I walked the streets, sometimes alone, I would walk and sing one of my favorite hymns; "Precious Lord take my hand, lead me on, let me stand, I am tired, I am weak, I am worn." Why God, why me? What have I done so wrong that my life has gone in the trenches! Day after day, I would return to the same insane behaviors, hoping that I would rise up out of the dreadful life I was living!

My beautiful, Spirit-filled Momma would ask me to pray. I remember those nights when I would come home from a drug run, and I would sit on the floor near my momma's bedroom and cry out to tell her that I was tired of living this dreadful life! She would always tell me that she was praying for me and would ask me to pray

and ask God to help me. I was so angry with God that I

felt my prayers were to no avail! Why would He hear a

prayer from someone who was angry with Him?

(Proverbs 145:8 "The Lord is gracious and full of

compassion, slow to anger and of great mercy.")

 You see, this was not all about me! I had a son

who desperately needed his Momma. When I would go

to my Momma's home he would be there and most

times, he would greet me at the door. I could always see

the hurt in his face. Oh my God, why me? Near the end

of my substance abuse, my son would see me and walk

away. Now, I was really angry with God. Why me, God?

 In August 1995, I remember staying up most of

the night, ironing my clothes and packing my bags to

enter a drug program. All I wanted to do was stop using

drugs and dying from its use. The God I had come to

know during these tumultuous using years was a

punishing God. Even though growing up from late teens

through adolescence, I had learned from attending

Sunday school, youth fellowship, and many other

sermons that the God I had known was not a punishing

God. However, the disease of addiction had embraced

me physically, mentally, emotionally, and spiritually.

The God I had come to know was a punishing God!

How dare anyone tell me differently!

When I entered that program, I wanted to leave

many times. Over the years being in and out of

treatment facilities and attending 12-step meetings, I

learned the Serenity Prayer. This Prayer was my comfort!

I would ask God to grant me peace so I would be still

and know that He is God, grant me the courage to fight

the demons that were telling me to leave that program,

and grant me wisdom to know the difference. Amen!

This was the prayer that carried me through. In October

1996, I graduated from that program! For eleven years, I

*remained clean and sober and eventually started
working in the field of recovery to help others like me.*

*In 1998, I married a wonderful Christian man; my
son proudly walked me down the aisle and placed my
hand in my husband's hand. My beautiful Mom stood
up and spoke of my troubles and how proud she was of
me! I remember her telling our wedding attendees that it
was only by God's Grace, she knew I would get through
those tumultuous times.*

*I thought my life was on track, but I did not
embrace the love for God. Instead, I went about life
doing my will and not God's will. My husband and I
would attend church together, but our marriage was
slowly dissipating. I did not take the time to talk with
God to ask Him for guidance. Instead, my husband and
I separated. Soon thereafter, I was alone. My son and his
family moved to Atlanta. My brother who was residing
with my husband and I moved to Texas. Where was*

God? I had placed Him on the back burner; not fully knowing that He was the one who was carrying me through the separation of my husband, my son and his family leaving, and now my brother leaving. I was alone! But God, why? You have brought me thus far, don't leave me! Not now when I need you?

(Deuteronomy 31:8) "And the Lord. He that doth go before thee, he will be with thee, he will not fail thee, neither forsake thee, fear not, neither be dismayed. However, I had left God to do my will.

In 2006, I once again did my will and entered into a relationship while still married. Knowing that in the eyes of God, this was adultery and wrong. This is what occurs when one acts on his will and not the will of God.

In 2007, I made the decision, (I place emphasis on "I") to use drugs again. I came so close to death. At some time during the night as I lay on the floor, my eyes opened, and I saw the dark sky. In that sky was a tiny glimmer of light. I want to believe that God was present.

I did not fully awaken until the following afternoon. I

was on the floor and I could not get up! I lay there until

my phone rang and had to crawl to the bed to reach the

phone. It was my boss asking why I was not at work. At

some time during the night, my eyes opened. My

neighbor heard me cry out for help that afternoon and

came upstairs. I was still in my clothing, fully dressed

from the day before. She called her brother to come and

take me to the hospital because I did not want anyone to

know what I had done. I was so ashamed and one more

time, I asked God, why?

When I arrived at the hospital, I had an acute

renal failure (from lying on my side on the floor for more

than 15 hours), heart attack, and a stroke. I was near

death. Many tests were run on me during my two-week

stay, including a CT scan of my brain. The doctor came

into the ICU and talked to me. He informed me that I

had an anterior venous malformation (aka AVM) in my brain; and if it was not repaired, there was a strong likelihood I would have an aneurysm. I was so aloof, none of this aroused me. I was so happy to be alive but yet frightened. I had so many people who came to visit me. Some prayed with me and others told me they were praying for me. I was on such a pity pot, filled with guilt and shame. The song in my head would come up "Precious Lord take my hand, I am tired, I am weak, I am worn."

These past eight and a half years have not been an easy journey. I have depression and anxiety. However, my physical and mental challenges have brought me closer to God. I am no longer angry because my God did not forsake me. He has been with me all of these past eight years. I ask God daily to lead me, lest I stray.

I continue to live with my mom who is 94 years old... I can truly say that I am blessed! My God loves and has not forsaken me. He is giving me strength, courage, and wisdom to take care of my mom who took care of me when I could not bathe nor feed myself, and who sometimes helped me dress. My son calls me daily from Atlanta, my husband and I (although still separated) worship together; I sing in the choir and he ushers. My brother and his wife live in Dallas and he recently celebrated his 72nd birthday, sober.

I am still standing, only by God's grace and mercy. I work part-time as a Peer Support Specialist with people who have mental and substance abuse challenges. "If I can help somebody along my journey, then my living is not in vain. I don't feel no ways tired, nobody told me that the road would be easy, I don't believe my God brought me this far to leave me.

This is my testimony. Thank you for allowing me to

share it.

Peace & Blessings

~Faye~

It is my hope that this amazing testimony of recovery leading to wholeness has blessed you. The temptations that this beautiful sister has had to endure over the years, though meant for evil and destruction, has managed to bring life and wholeness to someone today. God is truly amazing and never goes back on His promise to be faithful to His dear children. I pray this testimony will help rescue someone today and bring them to a place of complete wholeness.

HAVE A BLESSED DAY!!!

Day 18 Study Questions

How does knowing that God will not let you be tempted above your ability, help you to endure?

_____

_____

_____

_____

_____

_____

_____

_____

_____

_____

_____

_____

_____

_____

How can this testimony minister wholeness to you or

someone you know today?

_____

_____

_____

_____

_____

_____

_____

_____

_____

_____

_____

_____

_____

_____

Do you ever question God when temptation hits? Why?

Why not?

_____

_____

_____

_____

_____

_____

_____

_____

_____

_____

_____

_____

_____

_____

_____

Day 19

Complete Restoration Brings Wholeness

Psalm 51:9-12

"Hide your face from my sins and blot out all my iniquities. Create in me a clean heart, O God, and renew a right and steadfast spirit within me. Do not cast me away from your presence and do not take Your Holy Spirit from me. Restore to me the joy of your salvation and sustain me with a willing spirit."

This is a psalm of David when the prophet Nathan confronted him after he committed adultery with Bathsheba. David had previously walked diligently with the Lord and experienced the joy of the Lord. He now finds himself in the depths of despair, recognizing he had plunged into the sin of immorality. This entire chapter speaks of his prolonged time of repentance and the spiritual struggle he had to endure before receiving the assurance that God would restore him back to His good graces. Verse 5 of this chapter says, *"I was brought forth in [a state of] wickedness; in sin, my mother conceived me [and from my beginning I, too, was sinful]*". Therefore, it does not matter who we are, how long we have been saved or how close we feel we are to God, we have the propensity to sin. Prior to this crucial event in David's life, God referred to him as a man after His heart, hence, it was difficult for David to believe he could be restored back to that place of unity with his loving Father.

David pleads with God to hide His face from his sin and blot out, meaning having no recollection of his iniquities. After all, he had not only committed adultery but had followed it up by committing murder. David now gets to this point in his repentance, where he asks God to create a new spirit in him. All of us, as believers, need God to create pure hearts in us that keep us from constantly sinning and walking away from Him. Only God has the power to restore us back to Himself, but it is up to us to ask. David knew, and we should know as well, that if God takes that convicting power of His Spirit from us, all hope of deliverance would be gone. His request, therefore, is for complete restoration. Though

David was restored he had to suffer the consequences of his actions. The life of this Biblical pillar should instill in us to exhibit a holy fear of God about our choices to spitefully sin.

The testimony you are about to read comes from one who found herself in a state of disconnect from God, choosing rather to abandon Him. However, she made the decision to reunite with God in a time of unbearable brokenness and God in His loving kindness restored her back to union with Him.

Every time I see a ray of light it reminds me of hope. I've learned many lessons in my life, I must say, the hardest thus far was having faith even through the brokenness. When I looked around me that's all I saw, when I looked within me that's all I felt. Having faith and not losing hope requires a crazy action.... LETTING GO! My brokenness brought me back to US (God and I) the "us" I left behind.

I was at a point last year where I could not pray, could not read my Bible, and could not sit in His presence. I felt completely disconnected. I reached the point where I completely felt nothing, just numb. I had abandoned God and when some things came to an end in my life I realized how far I had gone from Him. The sorrow that filled my heart was overwhelming. The brokenness I had felt was unbearable, and just the simple thought of how I fractured my relationship with God left a pain in my heart. At the time I could not understand that God was pruning and shaping me. He made me understand the true meaning of faith. Christianity is not based on feelings, but is based on faith in your worse feelings and when you don't feel anything at all.

God in all of His LOVE restored me, I didn't deserve it! This smile today was bought for me by His blood, that I may be free to LOVE HIM! I always ask Him why did you restore someone who stopped

believing in you and talking to you? He answered,

BECAUSE I, your REDEEMER, your ADVOCATE,

your PROVIDER, your FRIEND, your PRINCE OF

PEACE, and your FATHER LOVE YOU!! A flow of

unconditional love consumed me and now I believe in

nothing but His love because growing up I knew of it,

but last year I experienced it!!

He restored me and I took back everything that

the enemy thought he could take from me, MY LIFE,

my PEACE, my JOY, and my PURPOSE. I always think

back to that day, if I had killed myself I would have

never been able to look back and realize how much His

love saves, how amazing His mercy is and how

unconditional His love truly is!! Even if tears may flow

down the curves of my cheek, I KNOW that everything

will be just fine. If I can choose one word to describe

this year it would be RESTORATION! I truly became

whole, the person God wanted to draw out!

~Sarah~

Although this inspiring testimony may have found

you in a place of despair and probably wanting to disconnect

with God, it is my hope that you have been encouraged to

seek restitution with the One who loves you best. Hold fast

to the unchanging hand of God my dear sisters, regardless of

what you have done, or how disconnected you may feel,

knowing He will restore you. It is only as a result of complete

restoration that you can be made completely whole.

HAVE A BLESSED DAY!!!

Day 19 Study Questions

How has God proven His restoration power to you in

your Christian journey?

_____

_____

_____

_____

_____

_____

_____

_____

_____

_____

_____

_____

_____

_____

What are some things that have happened in your life to

make you feel disconnected?

_____

_____

_____

_____

_____

_____

_____

_____

_____

_____

_____

_____

_____

_____

How will you reconnect with the Lover of your soul

today?

_____

_____

_____

_____

_____

_____

_____

_____

_____

_____

_____

_____

_____

_____

_____

Day 20

Waiting on the Lord Brings Wholeness

Isaiah 40:31

*"But those who wait for the LORD [who expect, look for,
and hope in Him]
Will gain new strength and renew their power;
They will lift up their wings [and rise up close to God]
like eagles [rising toward the sun];
They will run and not become weary,
They will walk and not grow tired."*

Waiting is one of the most difficult tasks God gives His children to do. It is easier to hear definitive answers like yes or no than to wait. However, the Bible clearly states that we gain strength when we wait. To wait on the Lord is to completely trust Him with everything in our lives. It is total surrender to His will and purpose for us. This is an amazing feat that can only be accomplished by those who are sold out to God, and delight in bringing Him pleasure. God promises that His strength will revive us when we get fatigued on the journey, as we sometimes do. The metaphoric eagle's wings on which we are to rise conjures up in our minds the scene of

an eagle as they are about to take flight. God uses the eagle in

this analogy as a result of its magnificent power to soar even

when facing danger.

Waiting appropriately makes reference to those who

were in anguish during a long and severe imprisonment in

Babylon and had no view of rescue but in God. The

expression to wait is related also to those of us who feel we

are frail, delicate, blameworthy, and powerless, and therefore,

realizing this, put our faith in God. The covenant or

guarantee here is all-purpose in nature, and applies to us now,

just as it did in the times of the Babylonian captivity of God's

chosen people. Webster's dictionary defines waiting as:

"staying in a place until an expected event happens; until

someone arrives; until it is your turn to do something; to not

do something until something else happens; to remain in a

state in which you expect or hope that something will happen

soon". In essence, it is to be in a holding pattern.

God knows that we sometimes grow weary and tired when asked to wait and, therefore, gives us the after effects to waiting as renewed strength. This mammoth strength develops in us the ability to run and not get worn out, to walk and not collapse. The testimony you are about to read is about a woman who travailed and continues to travail in waiting. Her only resolve is that one day she will mount up on eagle's wings and her waiting will not be in vain.

When I was asked to write about my testimony concerning the death of my husband, I was certainly willing to share, but I was also a little unsure, to say the least. My concern was the fact that I knew I would have to dig deep down within myself to explore the feelings I have fought so hard to bury: feelings of deep despair, darkness, immense pain, undeniable anger and much bitterness. This was the man I was to grow old with, the one who shared my world. I have fought so hard to overcome these feelings, but I think what I did was just hide and bury them. Someone told me by sharing my

testimony; it would allow me a chance to heal. I do

believe I need to recover. Although I have come a long

way, and have made many accomplishments in my life

since that time, it still seems to me that I didn't

accomplish anything. I am broken; I am still a bunch of

shattered pieces held together by tape. I love the Lord

and have continued to hold on to his hand through his

word which renews me daily. Isaiah 40:31 says "those

who wait upon the Lord shall renew their strength". I

have held onto this scripture for ten years, and I am still

waiting. Not sure what exactly I am waiting for.

Whether it is healing, finding out what my life purpose

is, or just how or when I will be able to love again

honestly. I wait still.

My husband passed away over ten years ago, and

I am still searching for who I am supposed to be. He

was my best friend, my lover, partner, confidant; we

finished each other's sentences with just a look. Even in the times I didn't like him very much, and he couldn't stand me, we still had an everlasting love for one another. Sometimes I think I even placed my love for him before my love for God. He used to joke with me saying: I loved him more than he did me, but I knew that wasn't the truth.

We were married for about 17 years before he died. We went through many struggles: drug addictions, hate, relationships outside of marriage, and having three children despite his sickness. There were enumerable crisis, in and out of the hospital. However, through it all, we remained together. My husband had sickle cell anemia and battled with it his whole life. Although he worked most of his life, his sickness would most times get the better of him. He continually tried to prove that he was ok, and just one of the boys by always trying to prove he could do things that he knew he shouldn't.

Always creating situations and problems that I had to either fix or undo. He was an easygoing kindhearted man that had a very hard time saying no. Everyone loved him and there were a lot of people who took advantage of his relaxed spirit. This caused a lot of problems in our relationship because I was always known as the mean one who could and most times would say no. I knew he had sickle cell anemia when I met him, but I wasn't entirely aware of what this sickness would bring to our lives. I was so in love with him that I thought I could deal with anything, and married him anyway. Of course, by then we had already had our first child, so there was no other option for us but to get married. Three children and almost nineteen years later I couldn't have imagined the reality that was soon to face me. But, God knew.

You see, I didn't grow up having a relationship with God or His Son for that matter. I grew up Catholic and was very confused about the whole religion thing. I didn't experience what the love of Jesus meant until I met my husband and his family. I came from a dysfunctional home with alcoholic parents, full of generational curses. My childhood was filled with tragedy, deaths, family addictions and much pain. There were good times, but there were a lot of occasions when I could have just laid down and died myself. I lost my mother at the age of 12; having already lost siblings and family members to murder and drugs. My father abandoned us a year after my mom died. There is so much that I have seen and experienced throughout my childhood that a child's eyes should not have seen. I was a child that was forced into adulthood almost immediately, totally by passing my teenage years. There was no one to teach me, or show me things I needed to know. Therefore, I taught myself and learned how to survive along the way, even though, I didn't know the Lord at that time. He was aware of me.

I didn't understand it at the time, but God had

chosen me for such a time as this. He knew, as an adult,

I would have to watch my husband deteriorate and die

before my very eyes and in my arms no less. He allowed

me to hear his very last heartbeat and see him take his

final breath. Losing my husband was the hardest thing I

ever had to deal with, and I knew death pretty well. I

was lost without a purpose. My very soul ached. Again, I

was that abandoned young girl searching for someone to

love me. Only now, I had three children who had just

lost their father with daddy issues of their own. There

were now two girls and a boy with no father. They were

all very close to him and loved him every bit as much as

I had loved and adored my dad. I was thrown into

despair. Currently having a relationship with the Lord, I

couldn't understand why he would allow me to go

through this. I was very very angry. I couldn't see a

future. All those years of caring for and providing for my family was all lost to me. I had no answers. Jeremiah

29:11 says, "for I know the plans I have for you,

"declares the Lord," plans to prosper you and not to

harm you, plans to give you hope and future". I had held

on to this scripture and others for years, believing God's

promises for my family and me. Now I was stuck, and I

thought: where are you now God? Who was going to

teach and care for my kids? I definitely couldn't. I was

filled with such loneliness, bitterness, grief, anger, doubt

and unbearable pain. I didn't want to go to sleep, and I

didn't want to wake up because I was faced with the

reality that he was gone day after day, I am ashamed to

say, that I was even suicidal. I used to cry out to God,

even scream at Him at times. Why? Lord. I was told you

should never ask the Lord why, but, I did over and over

again. My kids were watching me deteriorate and

wanting to die. God, however, understood my anger. He

used my eldest daughter's words to snap me out of it.

My daughter who had just turned 16 the year her dad

passed away said to me: "Mom, every morning when I

woke up, I was afraid to come into your room because I

thought I was going to find you were dead." What an

eye opener. I didn't realize they were experiencing the

same dysfunctional lifestyle I had encountered so many

years ago.

From that moment on I knew I was the only one

besides God that they had to take care of them. Now ten

years later, that same daughter is a college graduate and

a married woman. All of my children are well rounded,

hard working and love the Lord with their whole hearts.

Yes, they still have issues, and it has been a struggle, but

with God's great mercy and grace He is continuing to

bring us through, I am still holding on to Gods' hand,

and he is still holding on to me. I think of the song: God

favors me. The lyrics say:" Can't help but to give God

glory when I think about my story." Every situation we

*face and experience is to bring God glory; to teach us
something. I am still unsure about what my purpose is,
but I am still waiting. I am still hoping and praying. I
still face tough times, and there are still times when I
want to give up and ask God why, but those are the
times I have to remember God doesn't owe me anything.
Giving his Son to die on the cross for me was enough.
He has given us a spiritual armor that we must choose
to put on, God sends people our way, which even when
we think we may not be able to go on, His words spoken
through them can and will help us through. To God be
all the Glory.*

~Madalyn~

My prayer is that this testimony gives you the impetus
to stay in your holding pattern and wait for the change that
God has promised. It is my hope that your heavenly Father
ignites you with strength to take your eagle's wings and fly.
God has assured us that we will be able to run and walk in

this race of life because waiting on Him does bring complete

wholeness.

HAVE A BLESSED DAY!!!

Day 20 Study Questions

When you get tired of waiting on God what do you do?

How is this action accomplishing what God has

promised?

_____

_____

_____

_____

_____

_____

_____

_____

_____

_____

_____

_____

_____

_____

What are you waiting on God for today? How does this

scripture change your perspective?

_____

_____

_____

_____

_____

_____

_____

_____

_____

_____

_____

_____

_____

_____

_____

How does this testimony reassure you about the holding

patterns of life?

_____

_____

_____

_____

_____

_____

_____

_____

_____

_____

_____

_____

_____

Day 21

Recognizing God's Plan Brings Wholeness

Jeremiah 29:11-13

*For I know the plans and thoughts that I have for you,'
says the LORD, 'plans for peace and well-being and not
for disaster to give you a future and a hope. Then you
will call on Me and you will come and pray to Me, and I
will hear [your voice] and I will listen to you. Then [with
a deep longing] you will seek Me and require Me [as a
vital necessity] and [you will] find Me when you search
for Me with all your heart.*

Most commentaries explain that chapter 29 of the book of Jeremiah was a letter written to the Jewish exiles after two years of captivity in Babylon. Jeremiah gave them instructions about how to live and what to expect while in Babylon. He admonished them not to live like they were in captivity, but to conduct their lives normally, as though they were free. They were to marry, build houses, seek after peace for the city where God had placed them, realizing they would not be returning as a people to the Promised Land for another seventy years. There were those who were predicting falsely that this would be a short captivity, but Jeremiah compelled them not to listen to those lies. He explained that at the end of the duration of their captivity, a remnant of their people would sincerely seek God for restoration, and He would answer their prayers as a result of the plans He had for them.

Here is where the promise of God's plan is revealed to God's chosen nation, but there were stipulations. God entrusted His secret to Jeremiah, not just for the Jewish exiles, but for all who would believe in Him and all on His name. He had a future plan and He wanted them and us to know that it was to establish a future and not to cause harm. The future explains that though we may endure heartache and trials beyond measure, our time has not been spent in vain. Hope reaffirms that there is a better time in store for God's people who persevere to the end. To wait for that future without becoming fretful when things go awry is the security blanket that grants us peace in times of storm.

This future plan, however, does not take effect unless we seek after God in prayer with all our hearts. The Bible, in 1 Thessalonians 5:17 declares, "pray without ceasing", and here Jeremiah exhorts that continual communication with God in prayer is what is required to experience His plan for our lives. The essence of the scripture is that when God desires to move in a great way for His people, He requires them to move in a great way in prayer. God has a specific time and a specific way to answer the prayers of His people, and it is usually connected to His purpose for our lives.

When I look back over my life I realize every incident, whether good, bad or ugly has been a part of God's strategic plan for my life. However, sometimes when the fire gets turned up and I lose my focus the manifestation of the plan becomes skewed. When I woke up on the morning of Friday, January 8, 2016, it seemed like just another ordinary day. I had no idea what was about to transpire and how it would change the course of my future. My husband had been in rehab

for a few months and I had grown accustomed to living

single in my four bedroom house. The only fear that I

had was when a lizard would venture in for an

unwelcomed visit, which terrified both me and the

lizard. I accomplished my regular routine of rising early

to spend time with the Lord before venturing into my

day, because that had always tempered my day when

faced with adverse circumstances, especially at work.

I had a regular meeting that I would attend each

Friday with the principal and other leaders in the school

where I had worked for the past nine years. In essence,

it was a normal Friday morning, or so it would seem. As

I exited the principal's office I scampered through the

front office just to say good morning and visit the office

of one of my colleagues. There was a lot of whispering

going on, but I chalked it up to just another day of

gossip for the office staff and kept going on my merry

way. I said good morning, but it felt like I had interrupted whatever had caught their attention on the screen of their computers. The chief gossiper managed to raise her head swiftly from the computer to not only say good morning but offer a slight remark about me always wearing nice shoes. As I look back over the morning the shoe remark was extremely random, considering all I was wearing that morning was ordinary flip flops.

As I ventured into the office of the colleague I was visiting, she asked what would become the most riveting question: "where is your husband?" To which I quickly answered, "He is in rehab, where he has been for the last few months." She immediately turned the computer screen towards me, which had a mug shot of my husband, who had been arrested for drug possession the night before. My legs became immediately numb and buckled right under me as I collapsed into a chair *that was behind me. She explained that I was the brunt of the gossip that morning and that this picture had already been forwarded to many of my colleagues on campus. I was devastated, but I managed to catch just enough bearings to pick myself up and literally run across the campus to my office and lock myself in. All I wanted to do was scream, but my throat was tight as I put my head on the desk and allowed the tears to run down my cheeks and onto the floor. All I could think about was leaving that office, packing my things and walking away from Port St. Lucie, Florida once and for all. The embarrassment of having to face my colleagues for the balance of the year overwhelmed me and all I wanted to do was run and hide.*

I heard a banging on my office door as the assistant principal, who had become my good friend over the years, shouted: "I don't know what's going on, but I have a key and I am coming in." When she entered the room she was greeted by the puddles of tears that had gathered on the floor. All I could say, with a quivering in my voice was, "I am leaving this God forsaken school and town once and for all and I am never coming back." She looked at me with a blank stare and uttered some words that I would never forget: "You have been telling me about your amazing God ever since we met, so where is your God and how come you can't trust Him now?" This question came from a woman who had confessed, for the past nine years, the fact that she does not believe in God. Therefore, I had been summoned to prove my God.

I continued working and living in Port St. Lucie for the next six months. As I prayed, God gave me directives and utilized Jeremiah 29:11-13 and other scriptures to guide me into strategic places where I would meet new people who would help me focus on my future destiny. God had and still has a plan for my life and although I don't know the specifics, He had

promised me many years ago that it would be above and

beyond what I could ever ask, think or imagine. The

plan is still unfolding with pitfalls along the way, but I

take my thoughts captive every day, reminding myself

there is a specific plan and "it is not to hurt or harm me,

but to give me hope and a future" if I remain steadfast

in prayer.

~Sharon~

I pray this testimony is a blessing to you today as you

walk into your own future plan and destiny that God has for

you. Though the road may get rough at times, I encourage

you to hold on to the fact that it is not your heavenly Father's

plan to hurt you. He wants only the best for you my sisters,

but it requires constant prayer and feeding on His word, to

hold on to that plan recognizing the ultimate end is for you to

be whole.

HAVE A BLESSED DAY!!!

Day 21 Study Questions

How has knowing God has a plan for your life helped

you during times of adversity?

_____

_____

_____

_____

_____

_____

_____

_____

_____

_____

_____

_____

The Jewish people would be in exile for seventy years,

yet they were being told God had a plan; when has

God's plan seemed impossible in light of your situation?

_____

_____

_____

_____

_____

_____

_____

_____

_____

_____

_____

_____

_____

How does the testimony today impact your life?

_____

_____

_____

_____

_____

_____

_____

_____

_____

_____

_____

_____

_____

_____

_____

_____

Day 22

Knowing How We Are Made Brings Wholeness

Psalm 139:13-14

*"For You formed my innermost parts;
You knit me [together] in my mother's womb.
I will give thanks and praise to You, for I am fearfully
and wonderfully made;
Wonderful are Your works,
And my soul knows it very well."*

It is obvious from these verses that God aggressively cares for human life, from conception to birth. Even prior to a baby being conceived, God has a direct plan for that life. During conception, He specifically threads the fetus together till it becomes all He fashions it to be at birth. This is why abortion is considered murder in His sight, regardless of what the world may say or think. God puts together our parts as one would weave a basket, knit a blanket or stitch a garment. If one stitch is out of place it becomes obvious to the naked eye. He strategically forms us in our mother's womb, making sure every stitch is in place and that no two of us are exactly the same. This is a miracle that cannot be fathomed, but one that makes those who disbelieve stand in wonder.

Being fearfully and wonderfully made is a wonder that we must constantly praise God for. From the very core of our being God is involved and He does not make mistakes. If we are so marvelously made even before we are born, how shall we interpret the Lord's connections with us after we relinquish His undisclosed place of work? When He guides us, as believers, through our narrow path of life; what shall we say about our rebirth which is even more mystifying than the original birth? This new birth exhibits even more love and knowledge than the Lord can sever. The best we can offer is a high note of praise to the one we call Jehovah, Elohim, El Shaddai and so much more.

As I take another stroll down memory lane I rehash thoughts of being raised by amazing parents. They were not rich as some count riches, but they lavished so much love on their children it felt as though we were rich. My dad had the uncanny ability to walk into a room and create an atmosphere of laughter and joy. I recall him taking me to dinner often, just to let me know how beautiful I was and inform me that it was absolutely well with my future. He told me secret things about how I was conceived in love and was not a mistake, even though I was born twelve years after my only biological sister. I believe he wanted to instill in me the fact that I was valuable and never to be treated as anything less. He passed away in 1995, but his words linger on in my memory.

This Psalm always reminds me of those secret Friday night talks I had with my dad so many years ago. Though he is no longer here and was not able to share in who I have become, the legacy of his talks live on in me. Over the years since his death, I have had to face some gruesome circumstances at the hands of men who expressed their desire to love me. I have been married twice and on both counts, I desired that it be a lifelong

decision. However, the trials and circumstances faced in

those marriages, at times, made me forget how fearfully

and wonderfully made I am. The words of my earthly

father became obscure sometimes because of all that I

was facing. I recall years ago after going through a

divorce, someone sending me a card with the words of

this scripture etched inside.

While reading the card, I opened my Bible to the

scripture and the commentary below reminded me that

God is creatively involved in my development. He took

the time to accurately weave me together in my mother's

womb and cultivated every fiber of my being. Everything

I had gone through and was going through, He knew it

would happen, but made me with strong fibers that He

knew could endure. I was strategically made by God and

no matter how junky I was made to feel because of the

emotional turmoil I was in, He saw greatness in me and

I just needed to see it in myself. When I closed the Bible that day I vowed to live each moment knowing I had been formed and created by my heavenly Daddy for success and victory. With every discouragement I have had to face since then, I have resolved to remain whole because I know who I am. I am not a mistake, but a fortified warrior princess in the hands of Abba. I was created for success and victory in this life and will hear well done in the life to come.

~Sharon~

I pray that this testimony will help my sisters to rise to the occasion of being fearfully and wonderfully made. That one who sees ugly when she looks in the mirror should now see beauty. The beauty we must aspire to be is not outward, which only lasts but a moment, but the inner beauty that is lifelong. It is my prayer that you will read this today and be reminded who you truly are so you can live whole.

HAVE A BLESSED DAY!!!

Day 22 Study Questions

How does knowing you are fearfully and wonderfully

made dictate who you are?

_____

_____

_____

_____

_____

_____

_____

_____

_____

_____

_____

_____

_____

_____

When have you been made to feel less than who God

created you to be?

_____

_____

_____

_____

_____

_____

_____

_____

_____

_____

_____

_____

_____

How does the testimony today inspire you to know who

you are so you can live whole?

_____

_____

_____

_____

_____

_____

_____

_____

_____

_____

_____

_____

_____

Day 23

Clarifying Your Name Brings Wholeness

Isaiah 43:1-2

But now, this is what the LORD, your Creator says, O
Jacob,
And He who formed you, O Israel,
"Do not fear, for I have redeemed you [from captivity];
I have called you by name; you are Mine!
"When you pass through the waters, I will be with you;
And through the rivers, they will not overwhelm you.
When you walk through fire, you will not be scorched,
Nor will the flame burn you.

Many ask the question: what is in a name? People haphazardly select names for their children, not realizing they have branded them for life, and sometimes wreaked havoc on their future. As an educator, I have seen many names come across my desk and I often wonder what that parent must have been thinking when they decided to name their child. People usually go with what sounds good, or what flows well with the last name that has already been established. In Biblical times names spoke volumes as to who that person would become and thus, branding people with names was done very strategically and thoughtfully. As I glance across names of women in the Bible some names caught my attention, making me realize why each had to walk in the meaning of their name or at times change their name to accommodate their circumstances.

- Eve = to breathe or to live

- Sarah = lady, princess, noblewoman

- Ruth = friend

- Naomi = pleasantness

- Deborah = bee

- Mary = sea of bitterness, rebelliousness, and wished for child; beloved or loved

- Hannah = favor or grace

When we examine these Biblical women we realize that their names bore the significance of who they were or who they became.

In these verses, God reveals His love for Israel during their deliverance from Babylonian captivity. He lets them know there are certain benefits involved in that love, and the blessings mentioned here pertain to all who are God's children as a result of their faith in Christ. He explains that we belong to Him and He knows us exclusively by our names. The verses go on to make clear that when we go through trials and afflictions, we will not be destroyed because God is with us in the midst. Therefore, the waters of life won't drown us and the seemingly scorching fires won't burn us. It is so exciting to know that God knows our names and has a destiny for us that is invariably attached to those names.

As I ponder, today, the meaning of my name and how it is attached to my destiny and calling, I marvel at what God has done, but more so about what He is going to do. When my parents were faced with the advent of another child when my biological sister was already twelve years old, I don't think they even thought about the meaning and relevance that my name would have on my future. They saw this baby girl, born on December 23rd, and decided to give her the most popular name at the time. I remember growing up as a little girl in Jamaica W.I. hearing the name Sharon uttered on almost every corner of our neighborhood and in my school. Since then I have learned that my name, Sharon, has a symbolic meaning of a plain of land and a vision of beauty grace and love. As I thought about it I realized that vision is an inner beauty flowing outward and I had to work on actually living up to the meaning of my name. My former name, Ferguson, means vigor, force or choice.

Recently I have really thought about the names that I have allowed to be attached to me as a result of marriage. Smith means to smite or strike and Koen means wild goose. With this in mind and all that has transpired as a result of two marriages, I wondered if there was something connected to these names that maybe I needed to rid myself of so I could be free to walk as a woman of vigor with the fortitude to make her own choices. After twenty-seven years of not being a Ferguson, I suddenly feel the urge to reclaim my name. Though this becomes difficult as a result of the legalities I look forward to being Sharon Ferguson again one day: a vision of beauty, grace, and love that has the vigor and force to make her own choices. The scripture for today declares, "Do not fear, for I have redeemed you [from captivity]; *I have called you by name*". Therefore, I cannot allow myself to be attached to names that have served to keep me bound but must walk in the freedom to which I have been called. I feel a sense of freedom that I cannot explain as I contemplate the possibility of taking back my name. I recognize that clarifying my name truly does bring wholeness.

It is my prayer that today finds you in a place where you can walk in the true meaning of the name God has specified just for you. I think as daughters of the King we must embrace our royal names and walk circumspectly so we can be whole. Sometimes we may even need a name change (whether literally or metaphorically) to give us the courage to be whole.

HAVE A BLESSED DAY!!!

Day 23 Study Questions

What is the meaning and origin of your name?

_____

_____

_____

_____

_____

_____

_____

_____

_____

_____

_____

_____

_____

_____

How does knowing the meaning of your name help you

make sense of the circumstances of your life?

_____

_____

_____

_____

_____

_____

_____

_____

_____

_____

_____

_____

_____

_____

_____

How does knowing you have been called by name make

you feel about your destiny?

_____

_____

_____

_____

_____

_____

_____

_____

_____

_____

_____

_____

_____

Day 24

The Freedom of Forgiveness Brings Wholeness

Ephesians 4:31-32

*"Let all bitterness and wrath and anger and clamor
[perpetual animosity, resentment, strife, fault-finding]
and slander be put away from you, along with every kind
of malice [all spitefulness, verbal abuse,
malevolence]. Be kind and helpful to one another,
tender-hearted [compassionate, understanding],
forgiving one another [readily and freely], just as God in
Christ also forgave you."*

We are instructed here to rid ourselves of bitterness, wrath anger etc. The question immediately arises as to how one accomplishes this feat when the darts of indignation are coming from everywhere. The church has become a major target for gossip which eventually leads to hurt and culminates with anger and unforgiveness. The devil and his cohorts are constantly seeking to attack the people of God, in an effort to bring separation which diffuses to cause dissension in the church. We need to be extremely cautious to not foster a feeling of resentment because it can cultivate a basis for bitterness. This is why the Bible admonishes us to banish these feelings and embrace kindness, forgiveness, and compassion. The ultimate goal is for us to forgive others the way Christ forgave us.

When we think about all that God has forgiven us for it should make us stop and contemplate just what it means to forgive like Him. He doesn't just forgive, the Bible says He places the sins we commit into the sea of forgetfulness. It doesn't matter what we have done, He still embraces us and embellishes us with love. The ultimate sacrifice He made on our behalf was to die a sacrificial death on our behalf. When asked to forgive like God in Christ forgave us, it should conjure up all kinds of images in our minds. The first and foremost is the cross on which our Savior died. We have, therefore, been given a mandate to get rid of bitterness, wrath and anger so we can hold fast to a spirit of forgiveness. The testimony for today gives a vivid view of one of our sisters who struggled with the concept of being free to forgive. She gives us a play by play of what it took to finally surrender so she could experience the freedom to forgive.

Understanding and Experiencing the Freedom of Forgiveness

Some years ago, I had an experience in my life where I felt betrayed, condemned, ridiculed, misjudged and disappointed in persons whom I thought I could trust. These were people from my church where I had been a member for many years. It started, with what I described, as a simple misunderstanding in communication that was never properly resolved.

I recall how broken I felt. It was a horrible experience. I was going to church with great anxiety, being fearful of how I would be treated. That caused me to go with a defensive attitude and after a while, it felt like it was a waste of my time to even go there. I tried many times to deal with the situation, but it all seemed futile. One day I felt so overwhelmed because my mind was consumed with all that was happening. I had to ask

my friend to pray with me. That day I literally felt like

something left my body after we prayed. I felt free. I

thought that was my deliverance.

Unfortunately, after that experience, each time I

listened to feedback that was being said about me by the

people I trusted as brothers and sisters in Christ, my

wounds reopened. After a while, I realized my mind felt

contaminated again. I felt hurt, anger, annoyance, and

perhaps without knowing, bitterness was slowly

developing. This stemmed mainly from self-defense

because of what I considered to be false accusations

against me. I couldn't believe Christians could treat

each other so unkindly.

The saga continued for a while until I decided to

leave the church. I thought this would solve the problem

but it only helped a little. I was out of the environment,

but it didn't stop the gossiping nor my reactions to

them. *As I continued to focus on forgiveness, eventually
I realized that there were various dimensions to this
important, yet simple and frequently used word. In order
to forgiven or be forgiven, I needed to understand how
to achieve it and why it was necessary to do so.*

*By now I had been attending another church.
One day as I sat in the service, I felt the urge to meet
with some of the individuals with whom I had been
having the conflicts. Perhaps something was said in the
sermon that persuaded me. I don't remember. I also had
a significant offering that I thought I should give to that
former church since I had not transferred membership
and I knew they needed it as a growing church. I still
loved and missed my church family, who had impacted
my life so significantly. After all, we had many
memorable moments together.*

*I obeyed the voice of God or the right thing to do
and went to see them directly after church. The response*

was better than I anticipated. We got the chance to finally meet with some people. We discussed some of the ongoing issues that had caused unnecessary division, where it even impacted others who were not directly involved. People apologized in the meeting and it felt good. Even if we didn't agree on everything, it felt like there was respect for each other as we spoke. We decided to continue going to the other church because we started settling there, and we liked it.

Interestingly, among the lessons I learned, was that relationships may sometimes not be restored to their former state after expressing or receiving forgiveness. One has to evaluate and make decisions that are wise and best, as long as the motives are right. I also had to accept that I have no control over someone else's reaction to my forgiveness toward them, which if negative, should not hinder me from doing the right thing. Someone may also seem to revert to the state they were in before they apologized to me, but I still have to

maintain the right mind and attitude as I pray for that

individual. Most of all, I realize that forgiveness must be

MAINTAINED simply by guarding my mind.

~Melinda~

It is my hope that this testimony reminds you that forgiveness

is a freeing experience. There is someone out there who is

finding it very difficult to forgive because the wounds are so

deep. May this be a constant reminder to you of how God

wants you to forgive. Remember, it doesn't matter what the

other person has done, when you forgive they are set free and

so are you. Experiencing the freedom of forgiveness brings

wholeness.

HAVE A BLESSED DAY!!!

Day 24 Study Questions

Is there someone you need to forgive today? If so how will you start the process?

_____

_____

_____

_____

_____

_____

_____

_____

_____

_____

_____

_____

_____

_____

What does forgiving like God in Christ forgave you

mean to you?

_____

_____

_____

_____

_____

_____

_____

_____

_____

_____

_____

_____

_____

_____

_____

How is forgiveness a freeing experience for both you

and the person or people you need to forgive?

_____

_____

_____

_____

_____

_____

_____

_____

_____

_____

_____

_____

_____

_____

Day 25

Experiencing God's Care Brings Wholeness

Isaiah 49:16

*[The LORD answered] "Can a woman forget her nursing
child
and have no compassion on the son of her womb?
Even these may forget, but I will not forget you.
"Indeed, I have inscribed [a picture of] you on
the palms of My hands;
Your city walls [Zion] are continually before Me.*

The Israelites experienced many adversities and thus felt abandoned by God on many occasions. They felt the Lord had forgotten about them, but God gave them the heavenly

reassurance that He loved them with an everlasting love and

nothing could come between Him and them. This assurance

is to all who believe in Him and seek to live lives that are in

accordance with His will. He assures us that His love for us

surpasses that of a mother for the children she nursed.

Therefore, it is absurd for us to think that He could ever

forget us, or leave us alone, especially in seasons of desolation and hopelessness. Regardless of how it may feel, God's compassion for us will never diminish or become obsolete. No matter what it feels like God is watching over us constantly, with a love that cannot compare with any other love, we will experience in our lives.

The evidence of God's love for us is in the sacrificial death of His Son, who has us forever engraved on the palms of His hands. The scars left by the nail prints in our Savior's hands was imprinted so there would be a lifelong remembrance of His dear children. His desire is to care for us and love us for all times. However, when the circumstances of life hit, it is sometimes difficult to understand this love, and we are left wondering if God really loves us at all. The reality of these trials sometimes leaves us numb to the point where we become confused and wonder; has God left us to ourselves? It is during these life changing experiences that we need to cling to the fact that our Lord and savior promised that "He would never leave us nor forsake us" and He is not a God who lies. It is in these seasons that those around us will ask "where is your God"? and our answer must be clearly evident so they too may want to embrace Him as Savior. It is the prime time to produce yet another testimony of His goodness and the fact that He truly has not forgotten about us. He promised to be our Shepherd: *"The LORD is my Shepherd [to feed, to guide and to shield me], I shall not want. He lets me lie down in green pastures; He leads me beside the still and quiet waters. He refreshes and restores my soul (life); He leads me in the paths of righteousness for His name's sake. Even though I walk through the [sunless] valley of the shadow of death, I fear no evil, for you are with me; your rod [to protect] and your staff [to guide], they comfort and console me."* (Psalm 23:1-4) As I look back over my life there have been many times where the fire got so hot that I honestly felt God must have forgotten about me.

My life sometimes feels so confusing I just feel the urge to curl up in a corner and not even talk about it because if it seems ridiculous to me, I can only imagine what those around me must think. It was Friday, November 13, 2015, a morning I will never forget. I left my husband on the couch watching television and at about 3 am I was awakened by extremely fast heart palpitations. My husband had reverted to being a drug addict and the heart palpitations came every time he would disappear on one of his binges. Since I left him on the couch and I thought he had no money, my heart racing out of my chest was a surprise. I jumped up in a cold sweat and all I could think was God was calling me home that night. I crawled off the bed to the living room to let him know I needed to go to the emergency room, but you guessed it, he was nowhere to be found.

I called his cell phone to tell him my situation and he said he was at Wal-Mart and would be home shortly. Something inside told me he was lying and I was right because I laid there waiting about an hour before calling him again. At that point, his voice was slurred, so I knew he was on one of the many trips he had taken to the drug den since April.

There was an anger and hurt that came over me that made my heart race even more. He had taken my car and left me with his car that recently didn't always cooperate. At the time it never crossed my mind to call an ambulance, so I walked slowly to the car and drove myself to the emergency room. When I arrived I wondered if I would make it to the door, however, I managed to make my way and when the door opened I just fell on the chair. I told the person sitting in the front that I thought I was having a heart attack and they wasted no time stripping me of my clothing and hooking me up to machines. I could hear my heart

racing and with tears running down my face, I told the
doctor I was not going to die that morning.

I spent four days in the hospital with them
poking and prodding and finally finding out that I was
having a massive anxiety attack. As I lay in the bed day
after day looking up at the ceiling, there were times
when I wondered if God had forgotten about me. It had
been seven months of torture that I never bargained for
and all I wanted at that moment was to be set free from
this marriage. I had written a book titled "Christian
Divorce Wars" in 2013 and throughout the book I talked
about the fact that God hates divorce and so did I.
However, my body and my mind felt drained and for the
entire time in that hospital I never heard a word from my
husband until the day before I was to be released. He
called to ask where I was and I told him, but I think he
was too high to care. I asked where he got the money
this time and after hesitating, he told me he went into

my wallet and took my card and had literally spent $800

on drugs in two days. I told him he had to find himself

in rehab to get help. I gave him a week to do that.

Though my husband had disappeared during

that season in the hospital and I felt so alone, God made

me realize as I reached out to Him daily that He did not

forget about me and never would. Every night in that

hospital I curled up in His arms and just cried. He

assured me that those days wouldn't last forever and He

was right. Though I ended up living in my house alone

and the days were sometimes long and hard, I knew

God was with me. He gave me the strength to endure

and continues to guide me each day.

~Sharon~

As you go through your own times of hardship,

remember that God has not forgotten about you and He

never will. He cares more about you than a loving mother

cares for her children. You are the apple of His eye and no

matter what it feels like He will never leave or forsake you.

He has you imprinted on the palms of His hands and

experiencing God's care truly does bring wholeness.

HAVE A BLESSED DAY!!!

Day 25 Study Questions

When have you felt like God forgot about you? Why?

_____

_____

_____

_____

_____

_____

_____

_____

_____

_____

_____

_____

_____

How does it feel to know that you are engraved on the

palms of the Savior's hands?

_____

_____

_____

_____

_____

_____

_____

_____

_____

_____

_____

_____

_____

_____

How does the testimony today inspire you to endure

during times of adversity?

_____

_____

_____

_____

_____

_____

_____

_____

_____

_____

_____

_____

_____

_____

Day 26

Knowing How We Are Made Brings Wholeness

Psalm 139:13-14

"For You formed my innermost parts;
You knit me [together] in my mother's womb.
I will give thanks and praise to You, for I am fearfully
and wonderfully made;
Wonderful are Your works,
And my soul knows it very well.."

When God made us He took the time to strategically knit us together like a fine tapestry in our mother's womb. God is artistically and actively involved in how we are made, but as women, we sometimes negate this fact because of all the adversity we face and the negative things said about us, by those, who at one point, claimed to love us. However, it is clear from this psalm, that God made us flawless and took His time in forming our beautiful bodies. The psalmist metaphorically uses the word knit and when we think about a knitting project, we know that if one stitch is out of place, the entire project is flawed. The ambiguity of birth is one of the most awesome creative processes that God has put in place.

When He created woman He performed the first surgical

procedure to do it. In Genesis 2:22 the Bible declares, *"And*

the rib which the LORD God had taken from the man He

made (fashioned, formed) into a woman, and He

brought her and presented her to the man." This action

lets us know how strategic this process was, in that we were

not created directly from dust like the male species, but

planned and deliberately fashioned by a surgical procedure

like no other.

Though expressing the thought that we are fearfully

and wonderfully made was meant for all mankind, when we

embrace the thought specifically as it relates to women, it

should render everything negative that has ever been said

about us, or done to us null and void. This explanation of

how we were created should make us want to praise and

worship God for His miraculous creation of us. Elohim is a

name given to God which means creator and making us His

final creation is a definite indication that He saved the best

for last. In the beginning, when God concluded all His other

creations He said they were "good", but after He created

mankind He said it was "very good". When Adam saw what

God had done in creating the woman as a companion for

him, he stood in awe and amazement declaring, *"This is*

now bone of my bones, and flesh of my flesh; she shall

be called woman, because she was taken out of man." If

the men in our lives thought about us in this way it would

make it impossible for them to abuse us as some have. They

would, instead, be compelled to treat us with the love and

kindness God intended when He made us.

Though I don't think either of the two men I

married meant to abuse me, I still cringe sometimes at

the verbal abuse they inflicted and even more so at the

fact that I allowed it. Growing up, I was treated by my

dad like I was fearfully and wonderfully made.

Therefore, when I married I expected the same

treatment and I received it for a season on both counts.

When Satan came to visit the home uninvited, I saw and

heard things that left me speechless and hurt in so many

different ways. The end result was me balled up in a

corner thinking what I could have done to deserve such

treatment. I wallowed in self-pity and when I looked in

the mirror, I saw ugly where once there was beauty. I

had allowed the expressions and actions of men to make

me forget that I was fearfully and wonderfully made.

Sometimes I completely forgot who I was, choosing

rather to think of myself as nobody even though as

stated in a previous testimony, my name Sharon means

vision of beauty, grace and love. All that went out the

window when my ears received certain information

concerning what these men thought about me.

I recall some years ago when I was at my lowest,

someone sending me this scripture in a card. As I

revisited the verses, probing for answers concerning my

situation I remember the tears that flowed down my cheeks when I realized how meticulously I was made by my loving Father. It was in that moment that I rose to the occasion to choose to live as though I was truly fearfully and wonderfully made. I have had to revisit this psalm several times over the years so I could recover from the verbal backlashes that left me stuck in limbo sometimes. I realize today that if God took the time to creatively fashion me, then I should take time to cultivate wholeness in me, instead of living broken like Satan intends. I have come to a strategic place on my journey to destiny, where I have decided to live whole regardless of what I see or hear.

~Sharon~

My sisters, I beckon you today to realize that you are fearfully and wonderfully made. It doesn't matter what you have gone through, or are going through, God took the time to intricately form you, and He does not make junk. I know this day may find you feeling desperate and defeated, but I call your attention to the one you call Abba. He wants to be your daddy and you must allow Him to stroke your hurting places and make you whole. Recognize that it is only in knowing how you were made that you are able to conquer the negative things that have been said and done and walk in real wholeness.

HAVE A BLESSED DAY!!!

Day 26 Study Questions

When and how have you been made to feel less than

what God created you to be?

_____

_____

_____

_____

_____

_____

_____

_____

_____

_____

_____

_____

_____

_____

How will knowing you were fearfully and wonderfully

made make you live differently?

_____

_____

_____

_____

_____

_____

_____

_____

_____

_____

_____

_____

_____

_____

_____

Use this space to write to one of your hurting sisters,

explaining the knitting process God utilized to create

her and how she can embrace it to live whole. Read the

words out loud to her, or send it in a card today.

_____

_____

_____

_____

_____

_____

_____

_____

_____

_____

_____

_____

_____

Day 27

Latter Day Blessings Bring Wholeness

Haggai 2:9

*"The silver is mine and the gold is mine,' declares
the LORD of hosts. The latter glory of this house will be
greater than the former,' says the LORD of hosts, 'and in
this place I shall give [the ultimate]
peace and prosperity,' declares the LORD of hosts."*

While this scripture was speaking directly to the nation of Israel, it is also a reminder to us that though our former days may have been rough; there is a latter plan that will make those days look dim. The theme of the book of Haggai is the rebuilding of the Temple. It is the first of three post-exilic prophetic books in the Old Testament. The messages that Haggai brought were twofold in nature: to exhort Zerubbabel, the governor and Joshua, the high priest, to assemble the people to rebuild the temple; and to inspire the people to regroup and prioritize, in order to restart the work with God's blessing. The Jewish nation had faced some bad days and the time of persecution was not yet over. They had faced being in exile and so much more and wanted to revert to those days of living well when they entered the Promised Land. Haggai exhorted the leaders to be brave because their hard work was part of a bigger prophetic picture.

We too, as believers doing service for God in the kingdom, must take heart because there is a bigger picture ahead of us than what we are able to see in the present. God has promised great blessings and to dwell in peace with His people than ever before as our glorious and precious Savior. The world in its present form will not remain, only those who belong to God's kingdom will remain. We cannot look at our former or present state, we must focus on our latter house because God has a magnificent plan and if we waiver we will miss it.

When I moved to San Diego in June 2016 it was as a result of a dream I had in February 2016. The dream showed me that my family desperately needed me and because I was so far away I was unable to help. I could literally hear my daughter screaming at me in the dream, asking why I was not there in her time of need. The dream was so vivid I woke up with tears running down my chest. I immediately called California to make sure everyone was alright. My daughter asked why I was crying and though I couldn't really explain, I told her I felt God was calling me to San Diego to help my family. California was never on my bucket list as a place I wanted to visit, let alone live for any extended period of time. The only reason I had ever visited was because my children and grandchildren lived there. However, in obedience I found myself applying for jobs in that town, preparing to rent my house and sell most of what I owned to go on this journey across the country, away from everything familiar. I received word that I got a job and drove eight hours to Atlanta for the training. I was

*excited and a little nervous at the same time, but I was
also confident that God would take care of me. I would
rent an apartment and live in it with my son till God said
come back to Florida.*

*Arriving in San Diego was met with adversity on
many levels and the biggest of all was the job that I
thought I had fallen through. I immediately started
looking for other job opportunities, believing that with
my credentials it would be easy to secure a job. I was
very wrong about that as the rejection letters started
coming in and I was running out of money to take care
of myself or paying my rent. Each month I wondered
where the money would come from as I watched my
bills pile up and my funds depleted. I recalled many
times that this scripture in Haggai 2:8-9 played out in
my mind. I genuinely believed that there was a latter
blessing that God had in store for me and I didn't want
to miss it.*

Everything came to a screeching halt when I had

no more money left to pay for the apartment where my

son and I were living. It hurt deeply to tell him this, but

I had no other choice. I had been taking care of my

grandchildren every day since I arrived in San Diego.

Though they mean the world to me I still couldn't

understand the role they were playing in this cross over

to my latter day's blessings. However, as I sat on the

couch daily while they took their naps, I found myself

writing and being swept with amazing ideas of things

God wanted me to do in His kingdom. Though some

days were good, for the most part, I felt a sense of

confusion welling up in me. I could not explain my

testimony to my own self and shut down when questions

came from those who thought I should never have left

Florida in the first place.

My daughter informed me she was pregnant with

my third grandchild and explained how unplanned the

pregnancy was. God, however, was in the plans because immediately after she told me she became very ill and it was during her season of illness that I had to move into her home with her and her family. This was a very humbling experience for me, but I knew it was only another part of getting to the latter blessings God had in store. It has been over a month since I have been living with them, daily watching my daughter in her sickness and picking up the slack with my grandchildren and daily chores that she could no longer accomplish. In the midst of all this I have published another book, almost finished two devotionals, launched a Christian women's magazine and planned my first Christian women's getaway conference and so much more. Though my financial situation still looks dim, God has allowed me to realize that if I let go and let Him truly have His way my latter blessings will absolutely be greater than my former.

~Sharon~

My dear sisters in Christ though a lot has been left out of this testimony, it is my prayer that whatever your former or present situation is, you will embrace the fact that your latter will be greater; whether here on earth or when you hear your heavenly Father say "well done". I pray that this day does not find you hopeless but hopeful about what the future holds for you in the kingdom of almighty God. It is only when you look at your experiences, no matter how adverse, with hope that you will realize that contemplating latter day blessings really does bring wholeness.

HAVE A BLESSED DAY!!!

Day 27 Study Questions

How are your former and present circumstances

preparing you for latter blessings?

_____

_____

_____

_____

_____

_____

_____

_____

_____

_____

_____

_____

_____

_____

What are some blessings that you feel God is preparing

you for and what are some stumbling blocks to those

blessings?

_____

_____

_____

_____

_____

_____

_____

_____

_____

_____

_____

_____

_____

_____

Meditate on Haggai 2:8-9 and express what God reveals

to you concerning you.

_____

_____

_____

_____

_____

_____

_____

_____

_____

_____

_____

_____

_____

_____

Day 28

Restoring Stolen Years Brings Wholeness

Joel 2:25-26

"And I will compensate you for the years That the swarming locust has eaten,
The creeping locust, the stripping locust, and the gnawing locust—
My great army which I sent among you. "You will have plenty to eat and be satisfied
And praise the name of the LORD your God Who has dealt wondrously with you;
And My people shall never be put to shame."

There is no doubt that the children of God will suffer loss, sometimes great loss. However, Joel explains that we will be remunerated in ways that will blow our minds if we resolve to say like Job *"Naked (without possessions) I came [into this world] from my mother's womb, and naked I will return there. The LORD gave and the LORD has taken away; blessed be the name of the LORD."* (Job 1:21) This verse in Joel carries the literal meaning of locusts and cankerworms carrying away the possessions of God's people.

However, we can replace these insects with anything that has taken our stuff and left us feeling desolate and empty. The great army of insects was sent by God Himself to reveal to the people His power to give and His accompanying power to take away. His promise is one of restoration of whatever has been taken from His people.

We are promised plenty from our Father if we continue in obedience no matter what comes our way and what we may have to lose in order to gain Christ. Romans 9:33 declares *"BEHOLD I AM LAYING IN ZION A STONE OF STUMBLING AND A ROCK OF OFFENSE; AND HE WHO BELIEVES IN HIM [whoever adheres to, trusts in, and relies on Him] WILL NOT BE DISAPPOINTED [in his expectations]."* Thus, this promise is dependent on God's people exhibiting a spirit of humility and staying faithful to Him and His word. If therefore, we become egotistical and return to our old ways, God will hold back His blessings and judge us accordingly. When we adhere to His teachings and follow Him wholeheartedly we are assured restoration of all that the enemy has stolen and eaten away. We were created for victory and wholeness, and must never think we accomplished or recovered because of anything we have attained in this life. God has promised not to be slow concerning His promises, and no matter how empty we may feel at times as a result of stolen dreams, hopes and life itself, there is a season of compensation promised to those who endure.

I wrote a book in 2013 called "Weapons for Victory" and in it, I expressed a season when it seemed like all I did was suffer losses. There were moments when I figuratively buried my head in the sand and refused to come out for fear of another unexpected loss. It wasn't until I embraced the reality of this scripture that I was able to look up and see God in the midst of all of it. Though I had been saved for a long time, I saw new and different characteristics of God that I had never seen before. I recall on some mornings when I would go jogging, that I would literally hear the voice of God say "what I have in store for you will be above and beyond what you can ask, think or imagine". Though those words kept me going in that season of my journey, I knew there were other seasons to come and more mountains that I would have to climb in order for some things to be restored.

I am currently living in my crossover season and I am excited because God is about to reveal His great power in compensating me for all that has been stolen. As I look over all that I have been able to accomplish in the past six months with no steady income, I recognize the awesome power of God in all of it. He promised that if I remained faithful, He would "bless me indeed, enlarge my territory, keep His hands upon me and keep me from evil." In August I started re-reading a little book I had read over ten years ago entitled "The Prayer of Jabez". At the end of the book, the author challenged

his readers to embrace the Jabez prayer for thirty days

and watch all that God would accomplish in blessing

them indeed and truly enlarging their scope of influence

in ministry and life. I am currently on my 84th day of

praying this prayer. I have watched God do some

amazing things that I cannot even explain.

Though I am still financially unstable, He has

shown me that the things He can accomplish in me have

nothing to do with money, but just a keen awareness of

who He is and listening intently to His voice. I have met

amazing people in this crossover season which is a

testament of His promise that "my gifts would make

room for me and allow me to meet great people."

Though I have no idea where some of them will fit into

my future, I am grateful for meeting them and being in

their presence. The compensating rewards that I am

receiving and have yet to receive are allowing me to

daily write letters of thanksgiving to my Daddy God. I

know there is still a lot that I have yet to recover as it

relates to losses, but I stand in awe at this moment of

the great blessings my Father has chosen to bestow on

me in an effort to keep me whole.

~Sharon~

I pray that as you have read and digested this

scripture and the accompanying testimony, you will realize

that no matter how much it may seem has been stolen, God

is in the process of compensating you for all of it. I know

sometimes life seems so difficult all you can see are the sour

lemons that have infiltrated your life. My hope is that you will

join me in the Jabez prayer asking God to **bless you indeed,**

enlarge your territory, keep His hands upon you and

keep you from evil." (1Chronicles 4:10) I assure you that as

you continue in this quest God will surely repay you double

for your trouble in giving back above and beyond what the

locusts and cankerworm have eaten, allowing you to realize

that restoration of stolen years truly does bring wholeness.

HAVE A BLESSED DAY!!!

Day 28 Study Questions

What are some things that the locusts and cankerworm

have eaten?

_____

_____

_____

_____

_____

_____

_____

_____

_____

_____

_____

_____

_____

Where are you in the process of recovering your stolen

years?

_____

_____

_____

_____

_____

_____

_____

_____

_____

_____

_____

_____

_____

_____

How does Joel 2:25-26 encourage you to stay on the

journey to recovering losses no matter what?

_____

_____

_____

_____

_____

_____

_____

_____

_____

_____

_____

_____

_____

Day 29

Surviving Trials Brings Wholeness

Romans 5:3-5

"And not only this, but [with joy] let us exult in our sufferings and rejoice in our hardships, knowing that hardship (distress, pressure, trouble) produces patient endurance; and endurance, proven character (spiritual maturity); and proven character, hope and confident assurance [of eternal salvation]. Such hope [in God's promises] never disappoints us, because God's love has been abundantly poured out within our hearts through the Holy Spirit who was given to us."

In this scripture the apostle Paul lists sufferings as a blessing of our salvation. This word refers to the many trials the believer must endure during their earthly journey. The list is long as it relates to the different types of suffering as they may be physical, financial, neglect, grief, loneliness and so much more. However, as we press through these situations God promises to uphold us and keep us by His grace, if we consistently seek His face. When we seek and follow Him we obtain the sustenance to persevere and overcome these trials unscathed. Instead of driving us over the edge, these circumstances produce in us

spiritual maturity which leads to a hope that never

disappoints us. As a result of God's favor upon us, we are

able to look past our current situations toward a certain hope

in God. We, instead, grab hold of His promised return where

He will establish a new heaven and a new earth (Revelation

19-22). As we await this awesome promise God daily pours

out His love into our very being through the Holy Spirit,

granting us reassurance in our trials and a feeling of nearness

to Him.

As believers, we experience God's love in our hearts

as a result of the Holy Spirit residing in us. Poured out,

expresses the thought that we are in an existing circumstance,

which stems from something prior. Therefore, there is a

continuous flooding of the Holy Spirit upon our hearts that

stems from the amazing unconditional love of God for us. It

is only as a result of His undying love that we are able to go

through our trials and still be at peace. He gives us the

assurance that we have a future hope in glory with Him and it is not a delusion, but very real.

As women in the kingdom, we are given an extra measure of strength that makes us resilient during this fight for our lives here on earth. As a result, we make the enemy extremely upset when we rise to the occasion of the fight each day, determined to survive no matter what. John 10:10 declares: *"The thief comes only in order to steal and kill and destroy. I came that they may have and enjoy life, and have it in abundance [to the full, till it overflows]."* With this in mind, we have to equip ourselves to fight this superpower that wants to zap our strength on every terrain. Since we know he wants to steal our stuff and literally kill us, we have to remain armed and ready with the word and the power of the Holy Spirit made attainable to us y our loving God. The testimony you are about to read speaks of one of our sisters who recognized her for and was determined to fight for her survival.

Survival Mode

Survival mode is the mindset in which one is determined to live and rise in the midst of circumstances that have the ability to destroy them. As the years pass me by I continue to watch God transition me and with every transition, there are adverse circumstances. In the middle of every life altering situation I have had to make up in my mind that "I will survive". "I will overcome every burn the enemy has inflicted on me." This year, 2016, I have literally felt like Satan's ash tray, as my life has been torn apart.

I have asked God time and time again: "How will I survive this one?" I could literally hear God say every time: "Be still and know that I am God." A life of salvation is a life filled with life altering circumstances. The moment you make up in your mind to, not only survive, but overcome, the enemy torments you mentally and physically. With every burn, every torment, I am reminded that God is for me. I stand on flat feet, on a firm foundation, determined to overcome. The enemy may laugh at me, but every time he tears me down I get the opportunity to be rebuilt by my Manufacturer.

I encourage you to stand today, confident in your Father. Be determined to remain in survival mode, pressing toward the Promised Land, no matter what Satan inflicts on you. Some of you have been in the fire too long and the enemy believes and keeps telling you that you will not make it, however, I want to remind you that our Father, our Alpha, and Omega, has the ability to revive you. Hold on to Him and remain in survival mode, determined to overcome. Say assuredly with me: no matter what the dilemma, yet still I rise.

~Shanae~

I pray this testimony has given you the impetus to rise to every occasion of hurt, frustration, doubt and trials. God has equipped us with all the tools we need to fight the battles the enemy brings our way and win. My dear sisters in Christ you are survivors, but it is up to you to place yourselves in survival mode. Though you are in constant combat against spiritual wickedness in high places, I guarantee you if you arm yourself with your survival kit you will overcome and be whole.

HAVE A BLESSED DAY!!!

Day 29 Study Questions

What are you doing in an effort to fight Satan and survive every battle?

_____

_____

_____

_____

_____

_____

_____

_____

_____

_____

_____

_____

_____

_____

_____

How does this testimony encourage you to stay in

survival mode?

_____

_____

_____

_____

_____

_____

_____

_____

_____

_____

_____

_____

_____

_____

If you have not already done so, how can you apply

Romans 5:3-5 to your daily life?

_____

_____

_____

_____

_____

_____

_____

_____

_____

_____

_____

_____

_____

_____

_____

_____

Day 30

Surrendering All Brings Wholeness

Philippians 3:7-9

*"But whatever former things were gains to me [as I
thought then], these things [once regarded as
advancements in merit] I have come to consider as loss
[absolutely worthless] for the sake of Christ [and the
purpose which He has given my life]. But more than
that, I count everything as loss compared to the
priceless privilege and supreme advantage of knowing
Christ Jesus my Lord [and of growing more deeply and
thoroughly acquainted with Him—a joy unequaled]. For
His sake I have lost everything, and I consider it all
garbage, so that I may gain Christ, and may be found in
Him [believing and relying on Him], not having any
righteousness of my own derived from [my obedience
to] the Law and its rituals, but [possessing] that
[genuine righteousness] which comes through faith in
Christ, the righteousness which comes from God on the
basis of faith."*

Paul speaks here to the church at Philippi about what it truly means to surrender all for the sake of Christ. He expresses wholeheartedly his desire to give up everything so that he could live a life that is pleasing to God. He encourages them and us that if we really want to know Christ, we must be willing to abandon everything, recognizing them as worthless

entities as it relates to serving Christ. Knowing Christ, to Paul

meant recklessly abandoning all earthly possessions and going

after Him with a vengeance. His greatest yearning was to have

full knowledge of Christ and to experience absolute nearness

to Him. This was a desire to know the very characteristics of

Christ, in an effort to be like Him in all ways. He was

desirous of a union with Christ that produced pure

unadulterated righteousness. He wanted to know the power

of Christ's resurrection, which can only happen when one is

renewed and completely delivered from sin. Paul desired to

share in Christ's sufferings, which would occur as a result of

self-denial and be willing to crucify the old self and suffer for

the sake of Christ.

We were called into the same arena as Paul when we

made the decision to relinquish the world and follow Christ.

Our righteousness consists of Christ reigning supreme in our

very being. It is a righteousness of Jesus Christ, in whom our faith lies. In response to this righteousness imparted to us, we are exhorted to sacrificially surrender and be willing to abandon all to follow Him. This mandate requires a sold out mindset which doesn't come easily. When we decide to surrender all to the Lord we have to recognize that all hell will break loose in our lives. Paul's decision to surrender all came with an awesome price that landed him in prison on several occasions and ultimately ended in death. The sacrifices to be made are numerous but the eternal rewards are well worth the effort. As women, who are caregivers by nature, most of us know what it means to sacrifice. However, to live a sacrificial life totally surrendered to God requires taking up our cross daily, no matter how heavy it gets. Luke 9:23 explains it best by saying: *"If anyone wishes to follow Me [as My disciple], he must deny himself [set aside selfish interests], and take up his cross daily [expressing a willingness to endure whatever may come] and follow Me [believing in Me, conforming to My example in living and, if need be, suffering or perhaps dying because of faith in Me]."* This is an awesome mandate that cannot be taken lightly but must be followed to the letter when we decide to surrender all to follow Christ. The most important thing to remember is the unselfish nature in which this should be played out.

When I made the major decision to make a move to San Diego to help out my children and grandchildren in June 2016, I had no idea why God wanted me to embark on a trip to a place where I never thought about living. The transition was rough, but I wanted to follow His directives. There were people in my Christian church circle who thought I was doing the wrong thing and they voiced their opinion unequivocally. There were times when I sat in my house all by myself wondering if I was really hearing the voice of God. When I initially moved to Port St. Lucie, Florida in 2006, I recall God implanting in my spirit Jeremiah 1:5 and 8-10 "Before I formed you in the womb I knew you [and approved of you as My chosen instrument], And before you were born I consecrated you [to Myself as My own]; I have appointed you as a prophet to the nations. Do not be afraid of them [or their hostile faces], for I am with you [always] to protect you and deliver you," says the LORD. Then the LORD stretched out His hand and touched my mouth, and the LORD said to me, Behold (hear me), I have put my words in your mouth. See, I have appointed you this day over the nations and over the kingdoms, To uproot and break down, To destroy and to overthrow, To build and to plant." Those words have been riveted in my spirit over the years as I met with opposition from church leaders in Florida, who just couldn't understand or receive my calling. However, when given the opportunity to help I did so, but not as wholeheartedly as I wanted, because I became cautious about church and the people in it. Hence, my life in Port St. Lucie was

filled with obstacles and pitfalls as it related to ministry
and life, therefore, I viewed San Diego as a new
beginning.

Prior to making the trip, I traveled to Georgia to
train for a job with the hopes of starting as soon as I
arrived. Upon arrival, I was informed that the job was
not at all what I thought and had literally fallen through.
I had secured an apartment for my son and me and had
some money saved up on reserve so I figured I would
just apply for another job and with my credentials all
would be well. However, after numerous rejections, I
realized this trip was not at all what I thought it would
be. It was a call from God to be truly willing to surrender
all and follow Him. I felt somewhat like Jonah and San
Diego became the belly of the whale. I had been
running from ministry because of church leaders and
people and not truly embracing the destiny and purpose
that required full surrender.

I have to admit I panicked at first when my finances were being depleted and I was unable to pay the rent to help my son like I planned. However, I continued to press forward in what felt like a maze of decisions that I had to make. All my money that I had saved was quickly depleted but in the midst of it all, God was allowing me to accomplish unbelievable things on zero budget. I have also been able to help take care of my grandchildren who have become my first ministry. I made up in my mind to turn off the panic button in my brain and totally surrender to God and His will. I know there were and continue to be some people all around me wondering if I am crazy, or like Job's friends if there was something I did to deserve all my stuff. However, this leg of my journey has taught me how to say like the apostle Paul "for me to live is Christ and to die is gain" (Philippians 1:21). Some days have been rougher than others, but God has continually been abundantly clear in letting me know this trip was not in vain. As I

contemplate returning to Florida, I realize I must

accomplish the task God gave me initially in Jeremiah,

to uproot, tear down and build without fear. I carry daily

in my spirit the fact that totally surrendering to God

means everything that meant anything to me in the past

must become worthless, so I can bask in the gains that

lie ahead. Since as I pen this testimony I remain

unbroken, I delight in saying surrendering all to the

Lord brings complete wholeness.

~Sharon~

My sisters, I pray that this day finds you in a place of

being willing to totally surrender to the Lover of your soul.

Rise above your situation and walk circumspectly into your

destiny. I know the road probably looks rough and the

circumstances of life seem confusing, but I assure you it is a

call to submit to your savior. Be resolute in your mind about

living sacrificially for God and He will take care of the rest.

He promises that surrendering all will bring wholeness and

He is not a God who lies.

HAVE A BLESSED DAY!!!

Day 30 Study Questions

Where are you in your journey to surrendering all?

_____

_____

_____

_____

_____

_____

_____

_____

_____

_____

_____

_____

_____

_____

_____

_____

What are some things that still need to be seen as

worthless in order for you to experience gains in the

kingdom?

_____

_____

_____

_____

_____

_____

_____

_____

_____

_____

_____

_____

_____

How does today's testimony encourage you to be sold

out for God no matter what?

_____

_____

_____

_____

_____

_____

_____

_____

_____

_____

_____

_____

_____

_____

_____

Day 31

Experiencing Drought Brings Wholeness

Deuteronomy 11:13-14

"It shall come about, if you listen obediently and pay attention to My commandments which I command you today—to love the LORD your God and to serve Him with all your heart and with all your soul [your choices, your thoughts, your whole being]— that He will give the rain for your land in its season, the early [fall] rain and the late [spring] rain, so that you may gather in your grain and your new wine and your [olive] oil."

This scripture is part of the practical warnings given by Moses in this book where he writes his farewell messages to Israel. In this part of the message, he clarifies the fact that the Israelites as well as whoever professes to be believers should listen and pay attention to the statutes and laws of God. Though we no longer live by the law, it is imperative that we recognize that obedience to God and His word produces benefits in the long run. Therefore, it is clear that we are to love the Lord and serve Him with everything in us. The book of Deuteronomy specifies a "faith plus obedience" formula. It is as a result of this that we are able to become heirs to the promises of God with His full blessings. When we refuse to have faith and obey failures and judgment mount. The scripture emphasizes two specific seasons of rain that the believer must be aware of as fall and spring. However, it is as a result of the rain that we are able to reap and gather in our new seasons.

As women of God striving to live holy, we must realize that there will be times of drought. Famine can come in so many different ways, but we cannot get downcast in these times, but still continue to trust God. No matter what it feels like God has promised to send increase as it pertains to blessings. The exhortation for us is to be still and watch Him do new things and send abundant blessings. The command for us is to faithfully obey everything God tells us to do during the drought, and then He will give us a harvest that we can gather. The problem is there is no time frame set for the drought, so we, at times become anxious and miss the blessing. Deuteronomy 11:26-28 makes the declaration:

"Behold, today I am setting before you a blessing and a

curse— the blessing, if you listen to and obey the

commandments of the LORD your God, which I am

commanding you today; and the curse, if you do not

listen to and obey the commandments of the LORD your

God, but turn aside from the way which I am

commanding you today, by following (acknowledging,

worshiping) other gods which you have not known."
Therefore, the blessings await us only if we obey His

precepts, regardless of how long it takes.

On this leg of my journey, I have experienced

drought in many different ways. There have been

financial, spiritual and emotional famines, just to name

some. The most frightful has been in the area of my

finances. I have been completely depleted of all funds

where my bank account literally became null and void.

There were times when just purchasing a $2.00 item

became thought provoking because my purse was

empty. I wondered sometimes, how God expects me to live like this, and He would quickly remind me to be still. He held true to His promise to take "supply all my needs according to His riches in glory". (Philippians 4:19) This promise has kept me sane in this season of drought.

In 2015, I recall packing up my car after an event that I was asked to spearhead at a church. As I was busy packing a friend who was helping saw a book that I had written on the back seat. She asked if that was a book I wrote and I gave her the book hoping she would read it and be blessed. After a few weeks, she called to say how much the book was blessing her as she read. She said she wanted to invest in the ministry but was financially unable. I completely understood and thought very little about it after that.

While sitting on the couch in my daughter's house two months ago watching my grandchildren, I *saw a text on my phone from this woman, who had*

become a good friend, saying she was ready to invest. I

was completely broke so as she asked where she could

send the funds, I responded that I no longer had a bank

account and she would have to send it to my daughter's

account. I started praising God for the blessing, without

even asking the amount of money that would be sent. I

had gotten to a place where I was just grateful that

someone wanted to invest in me and what God was

planning to accomplish through me. The woman I am

referring to is a stay home mom with four children to

raise so I knew any amount she gave would be a major

sacrifice. I called to ask her what the amount was so my

daughter would know what to expect. She said she was

investing $1,000 and I was speechless. That was an

amazing day as God revealed to me that if I remained

obedient in my seasons of drought, He would

abundantly bless me. There have been so many

blessings since that, but my heart is full even as I write because this is a testament to the fact that experiencing drought can bring wholeness.

~Sharon~

I pray today that this testimony reaches into the recesses of your heart, giving you the courage to endure, even in your seasons of drought. God is awesome my sisters and will not cause you to fail but has all intentions of making you victorious. I encourage you to wait patiently in your season of drought and watch as God provides numerous blessings. My experiences in my journey from faith to faith have taught me that we can become whole during times of drought.

HAVE A BLESSED DAY!!!

Day 31 Study Questions

How has or is God revealing blessings to you during

times of famine and drought?

_____

_____

_____

_____

_____

_____

_____

_____

_____

_____

_____

_____

_____

_____

How can the scripture today strengthen you when

drought brings discouragement?

_____

_____

_____

_____

_____

_____

_____

_____

_____

_____

_____

_____

_____

_____

_____

_____

_____

How does the testimony today challenge you to live

during times of drought?

_____

_____

_____

_____

_____

_____

_____

_____

_____

_____

_____

_____

_____

_____

LOVE NOTE TO MY SISTERS

Dear Sisters in Christ,

I pray this devotional has been an encouragement to you as you walk through your daily journey with the Lord. Though I may never meet some of you, know that you have been prayed for daily during the writing of this book. God always has you on His mind and has made it clear to me that He wants you whole, so you can accomplish His purpose for you. I have given you 31 days to read, eat and digest. It is my hope that you will read the devotional repeatedly and pass it on to other sisters in Christ who may need to be encouraged in their walk with our Lord.

"Put on the full armor of God [for His precepts are like the splendid armor of a heavily-armed soldier], so that you may be able to [successfully] stand up against all

the schemes and the strategies and the deceits of the

devil." Ephesians 6:11

Love and Blessings,

Sharon

OTHER BOOKS BY DR. SHARON

SMITH-KOEN

Christian Divorce Wars – A Biblical View of Marriage

and Forgiveness During after Divorce

Weapons for Victory – Memoirs of a Perfect Storm

The Shepherd's Call – A Manual/Workbook for Pastors

and Church Leaders

NOTES

_____

_____

_____

_____

_____

_____

_____

_____

_____

_____

_____

_____

_____

NOTES

_____

_____

_____

_____

_____

_____

_____

_____

_____

_____

_____

_____

NOTES

_____

_____

_____

_____

_____

_____

_____

_____

_____

_____

_____

_____

Made in the USA
Middletown, DE
27 November 2021

53527323R00176